THE AUDACITY OF YOUTH

Tochi Okafor

Published in Nigeria in 2016 by Winepress Publishing

Winepress Publishing
NuStreams Conference Centre, KM 110,
Iyaganku Road, Off Alalubosa GRA, Ibadan
Tel: +234 809 816 4359 | +234 805 316 4359
Email: press@winepress.pub | www.winepress.pub

This publication is designed to provide competent and reliable information regarding the subject matter covered. However, it is sold with the understanding that the author and publisher are not engaged in rendering legal, financial, or other professional advice. The author and publisher specifically disclaim any liability that is incurred from the use or application of the contents of this book.

ISBN: 978-978-53799-6-9
A catalogue record for this book is available from the National Library of Nigeria.

Copyright © Tochi Okafor, 2016
Tochi Okafor asserts the moral right to be identified as the author of this work.

All rights reserved. No part of this publication may be reproduced, stored in or introduced into a retrieval system, or transmitted, in any form or by any means, electronic, mechanical, photocopying, recording or otherwise, without prior permission in writing from Winepress Publishing and the copyright owner. Any unauthorised distribution or use of this publication may be a direct infringement of the author's and publisher's rights, and those responsible may be liable in law accordingly.

Cover Design: Eugene Odogwu
Designed, printed and bound by *Winepress*

WHAT INSTITUTIONS AND YOUTHS SAY ABOUT THIS BOOK

"*The Audacity of Youth* is yet another treasure chest and a fountain of wisdom."
— **Federal Ministry of Youth & Sports**

"*The Audacity of Youth* identifies and bears witness to a force that must not be ignored."
— **Amb. S. T. Dogonyaro (OON, mni)**
Co-Founder/Executive Director, African Policy Research Institute, Abuja

"… empowering piece geared towards inculcating in the youth the required drive and courage to incubate their ideas and see it to maturity and materialization."
— **National Universities Commission (NUC), Abuja**

"This book edifies and equips you for success by changing your thinking."
— **Okara Daniel, Medicine, Babcock University**

"In its simplest form, this book serves as both a warning and a guide. It's a book that launches young people into meaningful living. It's powerful enough to inspire even the most lethargic of individuals to strive and work towards a meaningful life."
— **Joshua Odebisi,**
Business and Business Economics, University of Hull, UK

"In every epoch, race or hamlet, there will always be a voice through the journey of life reaching out to mankind for an altruistic end. In this generation and time, Tochi Okafor is that voice, *The Audacity of Youth* is the message inviting you to a cosmic cruise of global impact and productivity."
— **Akujuobi Uchenna O.**

"It's the fulcrum to the long awaited change and the catalyst to the actualization and achievement of the millennium goals. It's revolution of evolution."
— **Tyokase Lucy Sewuese**

"A well-articulated book, providing inspiration and direction to the clueless, whilst at the same time, repositioning the values of those seemingly on the right path."
— **Ebele Oputa**

"*The Audacity of Youth* is a fountain every youth must drink from."
— **Akorede Shakir, Kwara State**

"Tochi Okafor is a blessing to Africa. With *The Audacity of Youth* as a guide, any youth is certain to get to the top. This is a must read."
— **Rex Idaminabo**
Principal Partner, African Achievers Awards & Advisory Board Member, World Leaders Forum

"*The Audacity of Youth* is a launching pad for youths who yearn to make a difference in the world. It is the best gift any young person can wish for."
— **Amb. David James Egwu**
Co-Founder, Young CEO's Forum

DEDICATION

To the GREATNESS of a New and Progressive Nigeria and Africa of our time and beyond.

WHO CARES OR SPEAKS FOR THIS GROUP?

(Pictures of Nigerian youths waiting to sit an aptitude test for employment into the Nigerian Immigration Service on 15th March, 2014)

NIGERIAN YOUTH BULGE: AN ECONOMIC BOOM OR DOOM?

(Picture Source: NaijaVibe.net)

"Our continent is a continent of young people, and it is getting younger. By 2025, it is estimated that the African youth will make up one-quarter of the world's population. By 2040, half of the world's youth population will be African…This means that in the next fifty years, approximately 1.1 billion of the workforce will be African."
— **Dr.Nkosazana D. Zuma, Chairperson, African Union Commission**

CONTENTS

Opening Charge!   **11**
Foreword   **13**
Introduction   **15**

Chapter One
The Power of Youth   **23**

Chapter Two
The Power of Knowledge   **44**

Chapter Three
The Power of One Unwavering Vision   **60**

Chapter Four
The Power of Small Beginning   **77**

Chapter Five
4j-Model Paradigm-Shift: From Baby to Rescuer Generation   **95**

Chapter Six
Becoming the 21st Century's World Changer   **109**

Acknowledgments   **121**

OPENING CHARGE!

"Our answer is the world's hope; it is to rely on the youth... This world demands the qualities of youth; not a time of life but a state of mind, a temper of will, a quality of the imagination, a predominance of courage over timidity, of appetite for adventure over the love of ease. It is a revolutionary world we live in ...it is young people who must take the lead."
— **Senator Robert F. Kennedy**

"Youth are a transformative force; they are creative, resourceful and enthusiastic agents of change... Youth have demonstrated their capacity to turn the tide of history and tackle global challenges."
— **UN Secretary-General, Ban Ki-moon**

"The worthy patriots who made Nigerian Independence possible were young men and women in their twenties and thirties."
— **Former Nigerian President, Dr Goodluck Jonathan**

FOREWORD

Through the ages, young people have demonstrated their abilities to transform their nations by exploring their potentials, gifts and talents in the best interest of humanity in various fields of human endeavour. The future of a nation not only belongs to her youth but it is also determined by the visionary boundaries of her young people. It is more so because youthfulness comes with dreams, passion, energy, creativity and ingenuity which constitute ingredients for national development.

Unfortunately, the advantage of being young is appreciated more by the older generations than youths themselves, either by the way of regrets for the opportunities that were wasted or in gratitude for having made good use of the time and season of youthfulness. I have never seen a young person who utilized his or her time wisely and became stranded in the journey of life in adulthood.

Africa, especially Nigeria, is a youth-populated continent. Our universities and other institutions of higher learning cannot absorb all the students currently seeking admission for further education. Unlike before, there are more educated young people with various degrees in almost all the fields of study now. These armies of energetic and educated youths have what it takes to change the narrative of Africa. However, there is one important quality that seems to be in short supply among the youth of today. Courage!

This is one quality that gives life to other qualities and without it nothing works. Winston Churchill, the British Prime Minister who saved Britain from the crushing hands of Adolf Hitler during the Second World War observed this when he said, "Courage is rightly esteemed the first of human qualities, because it is the quality that guarantees all others." Having spent decades in the university system as a teacher and an administrator, I have also observed that it is not always the brightest students that eventually make the most impacts in the society. It is true that education gives one the power to transform one's world but if one lacks the guts to use this power to drive his/her ideas and dreams to the point of achievements, he/she is not really powerful.

The Audacity of Youth is not only well-written but very timely. With the crippling fear of uncertainty caused by the astronomical rise in youth unemployment and the severe market competition, the 21st century world yearns for young people who are not only educated but most importantly, daringly adventurous. It needs courageous youths who can set up successful start-ups and grow them into profitable organizations. It requires brilliant graduates who can brave the odds and sail through the storms of today's workplace without losing enthusiasm and effectiveness.

Tochi Okafor has done his readers a wonderful service by writing this road map on how to take advantage of youthfulness and face the future more courageously. It is a journey of self-awareness and inspiration. Read the stories, apply the truths, and enjoy the journey!

Prof. Julius A. Okojie, *OON*
The Executive Secretary
National Universities Commission (NUC)
Nigeria

October, 2015

INTRODUCTION

The history of the world's progress reveals that youths have been the frontline agents of political change, the powerhouse of the industrial world, the brain of the computer world and of recent, the driver of the mobile world, and what they would create or do next, nobody knows. But it is certain that the world as we know today is only a transition to a totally different world. Youths have always refused to accept things the way they are through the audacity of their dreams and revolutionary ideas and they have always been the dynamos of positive change!

The world stands still in the society of the boneless youths whose passions, energy, creativity, dynamism, radicalism and future have been bottled and mortgaged for a morsel of immediate gratification through the poverty of the mind. Youths who by themselves have become prisoners of ignorance; who have become too lazy to open their books, too busy to think, too noisy to listen and too weak to act on their dreams; who cannot see beyond the pleasures of the immediate environment or the immediate pains of unfavourable circumstances.

In such a society, nothing works because the powerhouse is locked. Nothing changes because youths have neglected their primary roles as the wheels of the industry, as the drivers of transformation, as the vehicles of revolution, as the engine-rooms of business innovations and as the apostles of change. In such a society, youths abdicate the driver's seat of their future to the government of the day, throw their power of self-determination to the air and finally, allow the government's failures and passivity to make them cowards of life.

History shows that people who have dared and achieved great feats in spite of insurmountable challenges of the time have moved the world, often before reaching the prime of life. It is astonishing to know what the singular quality of audacity has enabled youths to accomplish.

The revolutionary document which conveyed the sentiments that secured the independence of America from British political domination, of which, many historians have been referred as "one of the best-known sentences in the English language" containing "the most potent and consequential words in American history" was drafted by Thomas Jefferson at 32. What could be more audacious than the spirit and the golden pen of this young man?

Standing boldly on the floor of the parliamentary house with the matchless eloquence of a seasoned orator, Anthony Enahoro, at 30 only, stood in the midst of elder statesmen and fellow patriots, armed with the courage that only the young can muster, looked the British colonial government in their faces and moved the motion for the independence of Nigeria for the first time in 1953. What a youthful gut! He shut his eyes at the inducements and threats of the colonial masters and fought for the freedom of his countrymen.

Having wrestled power from the ruling political party, Lee Kuan Yew became the first elected Singaporean prime minister in 1959 at age 35. Without the endowment of any natural resources, the indomitable young leader changed the status of Singapore from Third world to First world country. What could be more powerful than a youth with a mission, a hunger for knowledge, a consuming passion for change and victory-or-death brand of determination? Such a youth was found in Lee Kuan Yew when Singapore needed a dramatic transformation.

Nigeria is in dire need of courageous and brilliant youths like Lee Kuan Yew who will redefine party politics and national leadership. Where are the Nigerian first-class young intellectuals? How could we remain cowards in such a defining century for Africa? How could we watch our generation die daily in search of jobs? Arise youth elites of Nigeria and Africa! Friends, it behoves on us to respond to this national call or betray it as it were.

At 28, Barack Obama dared and altered the long-standing history of the prestigious Harvard Law Review when he contested and became the first elected African-American president of the Harvard Law Review. In 2008, Obama again altered the history of America with his message of 'Audacity of Hope' when he moved the world to his direction by sheer power of oratory, and was eventually voted and elected the first African-American president of America after more than 200 years of the institution of American presidency. His election could be best described in the words of Nelson Mandela, "It's always impossible until it is done."

The story of Barack Obama is a metaphor for the emergence of an African economic superpower through the audacity of empowered youths. The 21st century belongs to the African world and I have no doubt that the key to the explosion of wealth of Africa lies in the hands of the courageous youths of Nigeria and other African states. Africa's continental destiny cannot shine forth until Nigeria becomes the most valuable nation of the world by the year 2030. Save your laughter, Obama was laughed at when he first announced his presidential ambition. Youths of Nigeria can make the most populous black race of Africa the most desirable nation of the world if only they can dream, dare and take personal responsibility in their various areas of calling. You can be part of this Rescuer Generation.

It takes a focused courageous generation to lay the foundation of the industrial greatness of a nation. "All nations," wrote Samuel Smiles "have been made what they are by the thinking and the working of many generations of men. Patient and persevering labourers in all ranks and conditions of life, cultivators of the soil and explorers of the mine, inventors and discoverers, manufacturers, mechanics and artisans, poets, philosophers, and politicians, all have contributed towards the grand result, one generation building upon another's labours, and carrying them forward to still higher stages."

The power of America as a nation is measured by the courageous contributions of her young citizens in all walks of life as scientists, business giants, entertainers, writers, programmers, politicians, industrialists, preachers, educators, inventors and so on. A generation takes over from where its predecessor stopped and hands over an improved nation to the next generation. It is also possible in Nigeria, in all walks of life, especially in the political field. Can we find a selfless, passionate and courageous political youth leader with passion for change among the present young intellectuals other than proxies of the old order? It could be you regardless of your circumstances of birth.

We need an army of courageous youths who can turn challenges and problems into big time opportunities in various fields of life. We need young entrepreneurs who can use stumbling blocks as stepping stones into success. We are tired of the Baby Generation! Timber-men are wanted! I extend my hands of fellowship to you as I welcome you to the herculean task of building a progressive nation that future generations will be proud to identify with as their own country and land of opportunities. The die is cast!

What is your big dream? It takes courage to drive a vision especially when you have to start from the scratch with nobody to help you find your footing; when you can barely boast of the basic necessities of life. It takes courage to speak of your big dream before an audience when you had nothing to show. However, you can never amount to anything without vision driven by courage and knowledge. Some are born great; some have greatness bestowed upon them but men and women who move and inspire the world achieve greatness through the audacity of faith in their dreams. Imagine Mandela staying put in a prison for 27 years and Martin Luther King Jr challenging the powers that be with the power of oratory because they both believed in their dreams of a society of free citizens without barriers. Imagine Abraham Lincoln going after his childhood presidential ambition after several failures until he won.

The Audacity of Youth is a message of the power of a youth and how that power, through personal and communal responsibility, can be harnessed and maximized by leveraging the resource-power of knowledge, of time invested in one unwavering vision, driven by dogged courage and stubborn belief in the possibility of one's youthful dream. It is a message of the power of small beginning; a source of inspiration and encouragement for young visionaries to prepare and act on their dreams right from school or in their present environments. It is the fore-runner of the Rescuer Generation through the 4J-Model paradigm-shift.

As a youth, if you can develop hunger for knowledge in order to expand your possibilities in life; if you can concentrate your energies on one unwavering purpose; if you can develop courage to start and act from where you are with what you have; if you can only persist until you win; if you can make a decision to place value on every minute you spend; then, nothing can stop you from reaching your goal of impacting positively on Africa. Youth is the time to define the future but if lost, can never be recovered again. Don't throw away the youth. It is the foundation-stone of the future and the key to Africa's rising. Become part of the solution by aligning your thinking with the 4J-Model paradigm-shift. This is the central message of

Introduction

this book.

Most of the stories used in this book are quite inspiring and challenging as well. I hope you will find them useful in forging your reality with courage in your quest to serve humanity with your gifts in any field of your own choice, to the pride of Africa. It takes faith in God, courage, will power and perseverance to prove your true worth, but the rewards are quite satisfying. One can also say that it will take extra courage and persistence to make it in Africa, especially Nigeria, given the infrastructure deficit and the high level of value-decay. But nothing can stop a determined youth from succeeding.

You were never born to Africa to make up statistics but to make a difference, to influence the world and leave behind undeniable noble footprints. Never allow yourself to go through life as a 'wandering generality,' but as a 'meaningful specific.' I am sure, by God's grace, you'll make lots of money; I know you'll live a long life; but knowing what to spend your life, time and money on will determine your place in the African history when all is said and done.

I invite you to join the Rescuer Generation today by taking a walk with me through the six chapters that follow.

Tochi Okafor

THE GREAT BIOLOGICAL CLOCK (YEARS)

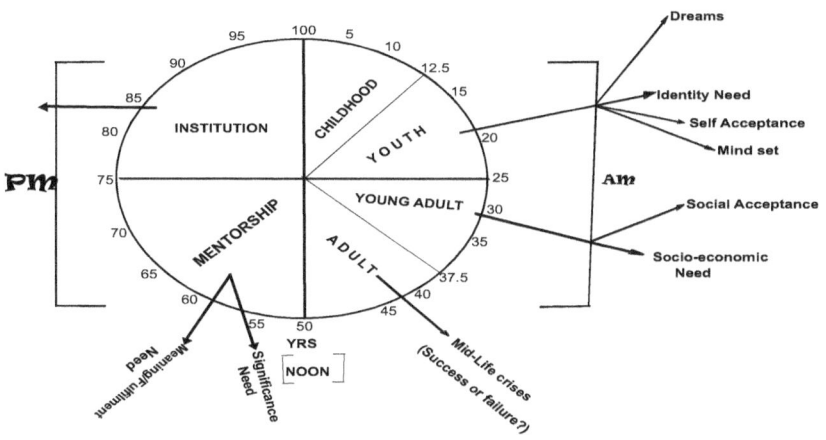

My dear teenager and youth,

The clock is ticking now ... wake up!
Thank God it's your morning of life
Are you getting ready for the future?
Today is your big moment – it's your chance to change the world!
Grab every minute and turn it into golden opportunities.
Don't miss your chance now; you'll regret it later if you do
I wrote this book to save you from this future regret
Let's begin the journey together here...

To your success,

Tochi

Chapter One

THE POWER OF YOUTH

Youth is a Golden Opportunity

At age 23, when Cambridge University was temporally closed down, Isaac Newton had, through private study, discovered calculus, gravity and a new theory of optics. He created his own golden opportunity!

At 26, the physicist genius, Albert Einstein had submitted a paper for his doctorate and had four papers published in the *Annalen der Physik*, one of the best known physics journals. These four papers – the photoelectric, Brownian motion, special relativity and the equivalence of matter and energy – would later alter the course of modern physics and bring him to the attention of the academic world. He created his own golden opportunity!

Before 28, Chinua Achebe, an acclaimed father of African literature, had written and published *Things Fall Apart* – a book which is not only a household name in the world but has also been translated into more than 50 foreign languages according to *The Washington Post*. He created his own golden opportunity!

At 29, Alexander Graham Bell had invented the first telephone and opened up a new industry that today controls our very lives by its amazing glamour and wonders. He created his own opportunity and opened the initial door of opportunities which the mobile industry enjoys today!

At 25, the first world oil magnet, John Davidson Rockefeller in partnership with his friend had founded an oil company later to be incorporated as Standard Oil Corporation which monopolized the American oil industry at a time through skilful acquisitions and was later broken into 34 different big multinational oil companies of our today, including ExxonMobil and Chevron. He created his own golden opportunity!

At 22, Thomas Edison had developed his first invention, an improved stock ticker which synchronized several stock tickers' transitions. The Gold and Telegram Company was so impressed that they paid him US $40,000 for the rights. With this success, he quit his work as a telegrapher to devote himself full-time to inventing. He created his own golden opportunity!

At 13, Bill Gates wrote his first computer program and by the age of 19, founded Microsoft with Paul Allen, 21, in 1975. They created a golden opportunity for themselves and for others, generating US $77.85 billion annual revenue with the staff strength of 100,932 at the close of 2013. Microsoft is the second most valuable brand in the world (2013).

At 21 and 26 respectively, Steve Jobs founded Apple with Steve Wozniak in a car garage in 1976. They created their own golden opportunity and job opportunities for its 80,000 employees who generated US $170.910 billion annual revenue by the close of 2013. Apple is the most valuable brand in the world (2013).

At the same age of 25, Larry Page and Sergey Brin, two doctorate students of Stanford University, commercialized their research project into what is known today as Google in 1998. They created their own golden opportunity! Google generated US $59.82 billion annual revenue with the staff strength of 47,756 as at December 2013. It is the fifth most valuable brand in the world (2013).

At 28 and 26 respectively, Yerry Yang and David Filo, two doctorate students of Stanford University, founded Yahoo Inc. in 1994. They created their own golden opportunity, generating US $4.68 billion annual revenue with the staff strength of 12,200 as at December 2013.

At 21, Michael Dell founded Dell Inc. in 1986 alone. He dropped out of medical school after his first year in the University of Texas and created his own golden opportunity. Dell generated annual revenue of US $54.94 billion with the staff strength of 108,000 at the close of 2013.

At age 12, Mark Zuckerberg wrote his first computer program. By 20, he founded Facebook with some of his colleagues in the university dormitory in 2004. Facebook has annual revenue of US $7.872 billion with about 6,337 employees as at December 2013.

The Power of Youth

In 2013, an Australian-born British computer programmer, Nicholas D'Aloisio-Montilla, after two years of undiluted attention on his pet project, at age 17 sold his iPhone app called Summly to Yahoo for US $30 million making him one of the youngest self-made millionaires ever. D'Aloisio was included in TIME Magazine's 'Time 100' as one of the world's most influential teenagers, as well as being profiled in their "Secrets of Genius" publication. He has created his own golden opportunity even as a teenager.

Don't Waste the Youth

You cannot estimate the worth of a youthful dream to the Gross Domestic Product (GDP) of a nation until it is allowed and encouraged to flourish. The UN and the Commonwealth of Nations put the maximum age of youth at 24 and 29 respectively, though the Nigerian constitution recognizes young people between the ages of 18 and 35 years as youths. In Nigeria, the average youth graduates before the age of 25. Some also finish their national youth service before this age, except those who may have to spend 2 to 3 years waiting for NYSC call-up. The problem is that young people in this part of the world think they are not qualified to work on their dreams until they have acquired a degree certificate and concluded their National Youth Service. The reason is that university education is appreciated more as a status symbol that gives one false self-esteem than a tool that unlocks one's intrinsic value as a person in relation to his/her true self-worth, self-significance and market value.

As a result, youth is wasted in the pursuit of a degree certificate (social status symbol) that would not guarantee automatic job opportunity at a blossoming youthful age when one ought to be exercising the highest powers of one's creativity with consuming passion while putting one's huge potentials to maximum use. At an age when energy and ingenuity surge at the highest level, instead of harnessing and channelling those creative juices towards a profitable end, even while in the school environments, our youths are waiting for WAEC, JAMB, Bsc, Msc, and NYSC as if success depends entirely on them.

At a youthful age when entrepreneurial spirit and aspirations are strong and blossoming, most of our educational institutions are seriously programming the minds of our brilliant youths for non-existent jobs in government, banks, NNPC, Shell, Chevron, MTN, Etisalat, etc. The youthful mind is never engaged in a rewarding long-term project that would unlock the creative powers associated with being a youth. Such creative energies are lost because of lack of personal leadership and absence of value-oriented mind-set. Apart from our anti-entrepreneurial environment for start-ups, this could be the major reason behind the increasing rate of graduate unemployment in Nigeria.

Youth is a window of opportunity that closes with each passing day. By 25, you may wake up to discover that it is gone forever. As a teenager, the whole world is before you for taking. It is asking you, "Can you dare me?" What you have before you is the whole world, not the whole time. I'd like to highlight here, the advice of Marcus Aurelius, "Do not act as if you had a thousand years to live." Instead, go after your dreams and goals as if you had only ten years to live and act as if it were impossible for you to fail. If you start now, you have enough time to put the hypothesis of your dream to test and before 25, you are either a factual success or prepared for great success. If I had known this as a teenager, life would have been different for me but I didn't lose out entirely. I started at 26. A poor fellow, you may say. Yes, you're right but don't repeat my mistake now that you know better.

Youth is a golden opportunity. As chronicled earlier, if you check biographies and records of other big corporations and big NGOs around the world you will discover they were founded by youths between the ages of 18 and 26. In 1992, the founder of three big universities and a multinational church in Nigeria, David Oyedepo made the same discovery. In one of his motivational messages entitled, *Dreams Secure Destinies*, he observed rightly:

"It is only in this part of the world that people never make a mark until they are sixty years old. I carried out a research in 1992 and discovered that if you do not accept responsibility in your twenties, you will most likely die a liability."

He continued: "From twenty upwards, you should be able to determine things for yourself. That means that you are considered responsible for your destiny from the age of twenty. From twenty, you must identify where you are going, and by thirty, the path must be so clear that there is no more desertion. Between thirty and fifty is your prime season. Whatever does not happen then becomes a matter of chance. To test the validity of this argument, if you check biographies, you will see that stars hit their brightest in their thirties. If you miss your planting season as a farmer, you have lost that entire period."

The Clergy therefore advised "...that between twenty and thirty are your visioneering stage. You should be able to locate yourself and by thirty, start proving your worth in your worthy purpose by driving yourself the heaviest towards achieving your goal."

If you lose your youthful season, you have lost your power and your entire life on earth because youth is the only planting season you have. In the 21st century, you are expected to discover your place in life as a teenager, if you intend to be a global player, because every bit of information you need is in your mobile phone and computer. At worst, you must make all the discoveries before you clock 25.

The Starting-Point

Consciousness is power. At this point I want to help you see your identity, opportunities, strengths, possibilities and your limitless powers as a youth. Not knowing what is possible for you as a youth and why you are a youth seem to be the primary reasons for high mortality of youthful dreams. Youth is not just an age bracket; it is a temporary time to *know* and to *do* certain things that will put you on the right track and guarantee the eventual realization of your big dream. Let's discuss the six most important things you must first consider as a youth.

1. Youth is a Time-Frame

Imagine there is a cemetery 1 kilometre away from where you are now and against your will, you are forced to go to this burial ground for your own burial. The good news is that you will not be buried alive because while you are moving toward the cemetery you'll be dying gradually and as soon as you hit the gate of the cemetery, you'll automatically give up the ghost. To help you make this journey, you were offered three things from which you must choose one – a pair of shoes, a bicycle and a Range Rover Sports jeep. If you choose the pair of shoes, then you have accepted to use your legs (walk or run) to make the journey and you must not stop until you reach your death destination. If you choose bicycle, then somebody else will ride you the same way as if you have chosen the jeep. As a youth with ambitions ahead of you, your choice (of using your legs) is clear because you don't want to die in the next few minutes if you were to be conveyed with the Range Rover Sports jeep.

The truth of life, whether you like it or not, is that you are already making the journey, not with your legs, bicycle or a luxurious jeep but with a jet because time flies - *tempus fugit*. Real youth is a time-frame of 12 years and before you know what's happening it is over, ushering you into a responsibility you never prepared for. The rest of your life from then becomes a struggle for survival. As David Oyedepo said, you have lost your entire life on earth and your children and the society at large will also suffer the consequences of your wasted youth – the most sensitive and rewarding period in life.

Still with our anecdote, you'll discover that a jet not only flies faster than any other means of transportation but it also offers a lot of comforts and luxuries. Youth not only flies but also offers a lot of luxuries and comforts that will make you forget that life is in stages and the higher you go, the more responsibilities you face. And as a matter of rule, each stage must prepare you for the next and there is no room for a repeat but for regrets if you fail any of the stages. Lost time (youth) cannot be reversed but can only be regretted! Imagine how much of youth that have been wasted in those two million applicants of immigration jobs and what Nigeria has lost because of unsustainable culture of government-led economy. Imagine if they had utilized their youth, maybe there is a Nigerian Bill Gates or Steve Jobs among those rioting young people with university degrees in the Abuja national stadium. This is not to blame the unemployed youths because I was in the same situation before I discovered a book that changed my perception and challenged me to take 100% responsibility for my dream in the face of daunting challenges. This is what I expect this book to do for you.

How much of your youth do you want to take advantage of before it evaporates? (Remember: it is a time-frame of 12 years maximum). As a matter of rule again: everyone doesn't have 60 minutes in every hour, 24 hours in every day, or even 7 days in every week. Each person only has as many minutes, hours, and days as he uses. It will pay you big time if you stop counting time and start making time count for you. Utilize every second and learn the value and power of a minute well-spent in a worthy purpose. Benjamin Franklin said that time is "the stuff life is made of." Wasting time is actually wasting life and it is not a murder case but a case of suicide. Don't kill your youth for it will determine the value of the rest of your life. If you want dignity, respect, success, fame and what have you, this is the time to 'buy' them with the currency of life – TIME.

The success of other remaining five things we'll consider depends on your understanding that youth is a short time-frame which determines whether the rest of your life will be an exciting adventure or a self-inflicted burden to yourself, family and society.

2. Youth is Your Most Important Season Whose Outcome Determines the Rest of Your Life

A season is an appointed time - a time with purpose. The wise king Solomon tells us that there is time for everything here on earth. A season is time for doing something and not knowing the reason for the season is very deadly. It is often said that when a purpose of a thing is unknown or unclear, abuse is inevitable. That's powerful! It means that if you don't know the purpose why you're a youth now, you'll definitely abuse it. Abuse simply means "an abnormal use." The question is: what is the purpose of youth? The better way to ask the question is: if youth is a time-frame for doing something or a season, then, what's the reason for the season?

A Season of Discovery of Purpose, Vision and Mission

At a point in my life, in the midst of loneliness, tears, disappointments, setbacks and crushing hardships, I had a strong feeling to call it quits and live like any other person. On the other hand, as I looked back on the number of years and investment I had made on my calling, I knew I will live with the feeling of defeat for the rest of my life if I ever quit. I have spent a minimum of five years in research - in search of an answer to the question, 'how can a young person who has no particular advantage in the world, start from the scratch and fulfil his dreams while making contributions to others?' I have written my first and my second book and series of articles on the back page of *The Guardian* under the column "Youthspeak," apart from other media platforms. I have featured in the network programs of AIT and NTA more than five times, and countless outings on radio programs including Radio Nigeria network. I have produced video and audio resource materials for youth development and motivation. Not long ago, after eight months of developing a program for the then Federal Ministry of Youth Development through the invitation of the Honourable Minister, the program was abandoned immediately the minister was removed from office. I was not given a dime!

Hope dashed, my hard-earned money wasted, precious time stolen and the most painful, I was totally whipped by the system that treated me like a slave in my own country. I felt disappointed that a country I was labouring to help at my own expense doesn't want progress because of the inescapable prevailing corruption in the system Things were terribly hard for me. For the first time, I doubted the possibility of my dream.

In this state of existential quagmire, something kept me going during those 'dark' months. It gave me confidence and moisturized my hope. It offered me meaning in the midst of discouragement. That anchor was re-invigorated confidence in my God-given purpose and mission in Africa. It was hard motivating myself. I could remember saying to myself, "*I know what I was born to do, I know why I am alive today, I know why I am a Nigerian, I know why I am an African. I was born to inspire a generation of young people that will make the greatest contributions to the development and growth of Africa. My path is unique and I don't have to conform to anything. I cannot leave my place of calling, no amount of disappointments, obstacles, executive snobs and rejections, financial stress or any man-made hindrance can stop me or displace me. I have made up my mind to win in this course or die trying to build a generation of young people that will think differently and lead Africa differently. It is a do-or-die affair. I have burnt my bridges. I have crossed the Rubicorn. I have reached the point of no retreat and no surrender – it's either victory or death. Forward ever boy! Oh I am a winner! Thank you Jesus.*" These words became my daily declaration.

I subdued the situation from within because I knew my purpose and mission just like I knew my name! I am pretty clear about the definiteness of my calling. I am not here to pursue illusory material wealth, fame and power; I am here to pursue purpose – I'm a stubborn courageous young man sent on a mission to Africa. The material wealth and fame are mere rewards, not the object of authentic existence. I derive my meaning and fulfilment from serving my purpose and advancing my mission - touching lives and transforming destinies. Apart from advancing in this course, life, as long as I am concerned, is worthless and meaningless.

It is your purpose that supplies you with meaning and fulfilment in life. Nothing else can take the place of purpose. It's like a life-buoy in the ocean of life. No matter how aggressive the storms of the tidal waves and the hurricane wind become, you can go to sleep because the end of your journey is peace and fulfilment. Yes, there will be shipwrecks, but you're covered already! After all, *it is not what happens to you that matters but what you do with what life throws at you. A wise youth is the one who knows how to turn adversity into prosperity; stumbling blocks into stepping stones and problems into opportunities.*

I have told my story for a reason. I discovered my purpose at age 26 and I got to pay heavily for it because I had abused my youth unknowingly. I had missed my true season for discovery. The price was high but I would still have paid a higher price with each passing year if I had not spent these five years for this ultimate discovery and preparation. It was hard but I did it hard anyway! There is nothing exciting and rewarding as discovering the reason you were born for such a time as this. Transforming that purpose into a vision and mission, and pursuing that mission with all your heart, mind and energy will place you among the top 5% that wield the greatest influence on humanity.

A Season of Developing Talents, Gifts and Potentials

To fulfil your given purpose, certain talents, gifts and potentials have been given to you to help you fulfil your mission. Though you were born naked, you were never born empty. It's only required of you to die empty at the end of your earthly voyage. What you were called to do (purpose and mission) gives you an idea of what your talents, gifts and potentials are. They may not be showing now but they are locked inside of you – they are your tools for creative expressions. However, there are some talents that are easily recognized especially in the entertainment fields; though they may be developed to make you a celebrity but if you fail to discover the purpose for the talents and gifts, you will abuse them. Remember when a purpose of a thing is unknown, abuse is inevitable.

Some celebrities don't enjoy the fulfilment in the midst of fame, wealth and power. You ask, why should someone have money, fame and power and yet not be happy? The problem is not external – it's that of internal disharmony or discord. It's an internal tension that could lead to depression and termination of life if it becomes unbearable. Disharmony of what then?

It is disharmony between your heart, mind and body. The heart is the seat of life and inside it is located your purpose in life – the message you brought to the world. The heart is interested in the core issues of life – its sole aim is to touch lives and make life more abundant for others. Each time it performs this role joy and fulfilment are sparked off within; the heart being the source of joy and fulfilment.

It is now clear that for any purpose to be worthy of its name, it must make life more abundant for others. Suffice it to say that your gifts, talents and potentials are not for you, but for the fulfilment of your worthy purpose. Where is the place of mind and body here? The mind and body are both mediums of expressing your message. That's where your talents, gift and potentials are located. *They are not actually to be discovered, they are to be developed.* The more you develop them, the better you become in your craft and the better you will reach people with your heart's message (purpose). I have been called to affect and make life more abundant for my generation and after with words of inspiration. This discovery just tells me that I have talents and potentials for speaking and writing for the purpose of motivation and enlightenment.

To fulfil my purpose, I must develop these potentials into skills with each passing day through reading, attending seminars in public speaking and workshop in creative writing, with daily practice in order to become better, if possible the best in the world. First, I will learn with my mind and practice with my body. The better I become at it, the more money I will make. Funny enough, if I am not paid, I will still do it because I am serving my purpose and my heart rewards me with joy and fulfilment.

Discord occurs when the medium (talents, potentials and gifts) and the message (heart) are not in alignment. If someone who is supposed to be doing what I'm doing now is currently working in a bank, he may be a good banker if he keeps developing his financial skills but he will be experiencing internal disharmony. His body will be there but his heart will be somewhere else. No wonder, Steve Jobs, the Founder of Apple, advised young people to follow their heart. The reason is that every disharmony causes disease. The patients in the hospitals are there because there is disharmony in their body systems. The psychologists deal with people with emotional disharmony. In essence, if your professional skills and your purpose do not align, you will experience the greatest sickness in life – heartache – many people suffer it five days in every week.

A Season of Sowing and Programing

A sick old man was dying. He had two sons. The boys had always felt that he had gold hidden away somewhere. He had never been a strong healthy man so his farm was not developed. At the back of the house, there was ten acres of stump land. When he was dying he said, "The stump lot." Again and again he said, "The stump lot."

As soon as the funeral was over, the boys said, "The gold is out in the stump lot." In earnest, they worked tirelessly in search of the gold. They tore up every inch of it. But they found no gold. Then the older one said, "We have the land in good condition, let's put in the corn." In the autumn, they found in the ripened corn, the gold.

You have a stump land in you. Out of this 'fertile land' every good thing you now see in the world was mined, including this book, your phone and your computer. Without this 'fertile land,' diamond, gold and oil mined from the ground would remain crude and may not be of much value to the world. This 'fertile land' is your mind. It was given to you brand new with nothing in it. From birth till now, a lot of stumps have been planted on it by the society and your environment. The way you think and behave until now is a product of what has been sown in your mind.

First, you discover your purpose and turn it into a mission. The next thing is that you must decide how far you can go in that field. Your purpose gives you a direction in the ocean of life like a compass but how far you can go in that direction is a function of your vision. The general rule here says, "As far as your eyes can see." There is no limit to the height you can attain in life once you're in your place of purpose fuelled with passion and propelled by unwavering faith in God, in yourself and in your abilities. In essence, it is not enough to discover your purpose and potentials, you must dream big boy! Dreamers are leaders in every field of life.

In one of my leadership seminars at the Nnamdi Azikiwe University, Awka, I was discussing dream with the students. I presumed that everyone in the audience understands the kind of dream I was talking about until a final-year student stood to ask a very funny but serious question as far as he was concerned. Immediately he started narrating the dream he had the previous night, the audience broke into uncontrollable laughter. It dawned on me that I have over-estimated my youth audience. Here, I also assume that you know that I'm talking about day-dreaming.

Dream is a picture of the future that produces passion in you. I find John Maxwell's definition more elaborate. He defined dream as "an inspiring picture of the future that energizes your mind, will, and emotions, empowering you to do everything you can to achieve it. A dream worth pursuing is a picture and blueprint of a person's purpose and potential," For Sharon Hull, "A dream is the seed of possibility planted in the soul of a human being, which calls him to pursue a unique path to the realization of his purpose."

A big dream is a seed of what you think is possible for you in life. It is not enough to think it, you must believe it before you can achieve it with time. You must not only sow this seed of possibility in your mind, you must program your mind with it until it becomes an installed program that runs in your belief system. Before April 1954, nobody ever believed that a mile can be covered in four minutes. As far as the world was concerned, it was an impossible task until Roger Bannister did it. Today, thousands of athletes have exceeded this target. It was a problem of belief system, not impossibility problem. All things are possible to anyone who believes, the Bible reminds us.

Program your mind with your dream and it will become your future reality. It is good for me to tell you that great corporations of the world today were born out of the audacity of youthful dreams that seemed impossible in the beginning. Again with emphasis, program your mind with your dream. This is how to create your own future and reality. This is the right season to do so. It is your sole responsibility!

3. Youth is an Awesome Responsibility

Youth is a time-frame and a season. If you do nothing now, it will surely slip away. If you want to command respect in future, you must do something now. For the fact that you have read this book to this point, I am sure you want to be somebody in future. Immediately you start putting it into practice, you start becoming somebody. Benjamin Franklin said, "One today is worth two tomorrows: what I am to be, I am now becoming." The truth of life is that the way you live your youth today is preparing you for tomorrow. The question is: "What are you preparing for? Are you grooming yourself for success or failure?" Are you preparing for joblessness or entrepreneurial exploits? You see, success or failure doesn't occur one day. Each is a process. Youth is preparing you for either success or failure.

Youth is an awesome responsibility. The rule of life is that there is a playing and paying time. You determine when to do any. You can pay now and play later, or you can play now and pay later. But either way, you are going to pay. You are at liberty to play (watch all the movies and catch all the fun) and do what you want with your youth, but if you do, your adult life will be harder, full of frustrations and regrets. You may have been born into a wealthy family or have powerful connections, but without taking responsibility, you are of no value to your generation and the world. However, if you take responsibility as a youth, on the front end, then you will not only reap a glorious and successful future but you'll be one of the most needed of this century.

The only adequate preparation for adult life is the right use of youth. At age 17, John Maxwell started taking responsibility for what he will become in future – a preacher, speaker and a writer. Today the 70-year-old-best-seller author with more than fifty books is America's expert on leadership, who speaks to hundreds of thousands of people each year. He didn't become an expert in one day as he recalled in his book, *Today Matters*, thus:

> *"From the time I was seventeen, I knew I was going to become a pastor. I knew that meant I would be writing and speaking to people every week of my life. If you've ever needed to write and present more than one hundred new lessons in a year, you know how hard it is to find good fresh material for an audience.*
>
> *In 1964, I started the regular discipline of reading with an eye for finding good quotes, ideas, and illustrations for sermon and lessons. As I found good material (on any subject), I'd cut it out, decide what topic best described it, and file it away. That's something I have done every day for forty years!*
>
> *Is it fun to do? Not especially. Often the practice is quite tedious. Does it work? Absolutely. The twelve hundred files in my office containing thousands of quotes are evidence of its success. Any*

time I need to write a lecture or want to work on a chapter for a book, instead of spending countless hours over the course of several weeks searching for high-quality material, I go to my files, and in minutes I put my hands on great quotes and stories I've collected. I simply look at reading and filing as a price I pay every day to make tomorrow better. It's a way of preparing to succeed."

Frankly, I regret my youth each time I read something like this but such story challenges me to develop a sense of urgency. At age 26 when I discovered that I will spend the rest of my life writing and speaking to inspire generations of youths, I swung into action like a hungry lion. I made a decision to be among the top five motivational speakers in the world by 2020. A big dream you may say. Yes, but a bigger responsibility. I started reading every work on personal development that I could lay my hands on – sometimes researching throughout the night. On several occasions, I was asked if I was writing a doctoral thesis. And that has fondly earned me the title of 'Prof.' among my friends and acquaintances. During my national youth service in Abuja, fellow corp members always asked me what professional course I was reading for. They couldn't understand I wasn't preparing for any exam. I was preparing for my defined future. I said 'defined future' because the fact that you are reading for an exam doesn't translate to preparing you for the future. The millions of job seekers, who are desperate to work at any job available, at one time or the other read and passed exams. You must have a clear idea of you want and let your preparations get you there.

In July 2012, it was reported in various national dailies in Nigeria that Dangote Group received more than 13,000 job applications for the position of executive truck drivers. Out of this scaring figure chasing 100 vacancies, 6 were PhD holders, 704 Masters Degree holders and more than 8,000 of the applicants had first degrees. You prepare for a definite future you have carved out for yourself. You don't just read to prepare for exams, you read because you want to create value with your knowledge in your discovered field of endeavour. That's education. I read almost all the time because I wanted to recover my lost youth. For me, taking responsibility for my dream at that early stage was a battle I had to win. Sure, it has paid off. If I had missed that second chance, the rest of my life would be a matter of chance.

Taking responsibility for your future gives you confidence as you march forward into adult life. Have you ever studied so well for an exam that you walked into the classroom with absolute confidence, knowing you would ace the test? Or have you ever rehearsed a poem thoroughly that you just knew you would be able to deliver as soon as you hit the stage no matter who is seated before you? Responsibility gives you that kind of feeling and mind-set, regardless of the challenges before you. You can so prepare for your dream that you can walk into the future with absolute confidence that you'll make it to the top of your field. As you take 100% responsibility for your adult life, I want to leave you with this advice of a 19th century British Prime Minister, Benjamin Disraeli, who said, "The secret of success in life is for a man to be ready for his time when it comes." Luck is what happens when preparedness meets opportunity. Become a lucky youth today!

4. Youth is the Most Reliable Predictor of the Future

Youth is a time-frame, a season, an awesome responsibility and the accurate predictor of the future. Youth is a promising future. It is a great prophecy about to happen. The presence of the great inspires greatness but the presence of youth assures everyone of something greater. As a parent, you believe that your children will be greater than you. An illiterate father can go to any length to ensure his son gets sufficient education. Unfortunately, not every youth fulfils this prophecy of a better tomorrow. You can tell who and who can make it tomorrow by how they think as youths and what they do today with the window of opportunity youth offers.

At national level, you can predict the future of a country by looking at her youths. If you change the youths' mind-sets, then you have altered the future of that country for the better. For this reason, I believe that a better Africa lies in better African youths. A producing and manufacturing youth will deliver an industrial Africa. The result does not lie with today, it will show as they develop into adults to pilot the affairs of nations and industries. You can predict the future of a youth and a nation accurately!

You can only predict the future of a nation by creating it right now. You create your future and that of Africa by putting into practice what we have discussed until now. Find out your purpose in life and make it a mission. Develop your potentials and gifts, and program your mind with the product of your imagination – your big dream. By taking 100% responsibility for your dream, you are not only predicting your future but you're making your future real. You are becoming a man of valour! You are becoming a lady to watch out for and a sought-after personality by people of substance in the nearest future!

5. Youth is a Divine Idea Whose Time Has Come

"...Know for certain that your descendants will be strangers in a country not their own, and they will be enslaved and mistreated four hundred years. But I will punish the nation they serve as slaves, and afterward they will come out with great possessions" (Gen.15:13-14 NIV)

A 17-year-old youth had a dream that one day he will be in a position of authority where his elder brothers, including his father, will serve and revere him. Out of excitement which follows every big dream initially, Joseph called his elder brothers and shared his great dream with them. The story of his big dream put him into series of problems when his brothers nurtured in their wicked hearts how best to eliminate the dreamer and the big dream. We were told that the dream landed the youth into a pit and eventually into a foreign land as a slave. As a slave servant, the dreamer's idea eventually put him into a prison but the sweetest part of the story of this young man was that his God-given talents of interpreting dreams delivered him from the prison and placed him at the highest position in Egypt after Pharaoh, at age 30. (How powerful are your talents, gifts and potentials as great tools to make your dream a reality! Develop them and nothing will stop you).

It was a 13 years of painful journey into greatness. What the youth dreamer did not know was that his youthful dream was a fulfilment of a great prophecy given to his great grandfather, Abraham, in our opening quote even before his grandfather (Isaac) and father (Jacob) were born. It was the Creator's idea that one day the people of Israel will move into Egypt and eventually be enslaved when they multiply into a multitude of nations. The youthful dream of this poor boy was a means to make this happen and no external force could stop it because youth is a divine idea whose time has come.

It is often said that there is nothing as powerful as an idea whose time has come. You are an idea whose time has come and there is nothing as powerful as your dream if you're in your place of purpose because you're a product of Divine idea. If you follow this biblical story of Israel further, you will discover that they eventually became slaves in Egypt after the death of Joseph and were heavily afflicted by the reigning Pharaoh who did not know Joseph.

Again, Moses was born and sent as a divine idea to bring the people out of the land of slavery with great possessions. There was a great scheme to eliminate Moses as a male child but as we have seen and proven already, you now know that no external force can stop the idea whose time has come. After 40 years of preparation in the wilderness, Moses led Israel out of Egypt with great possessions.

If you have followed my argument from the beginning of this book till now, you will agree with me that *youth is a person on a mission to solve a particular problem in a particular generation for a particular people living in a particular place on the world's map*. A Nigerian elder statesman, Maitama Sule who became a commissioner of the Federal Republic of Nigeria around about the age of 24, rightly observed in his interview with *The Guardian* that, "The youths are the vehicles and answer, the solutions and the vanguards of revolution."

I want you to start seeing yourself as a solution to a particular problem and an answer to a question on the lips of this generation. You are an agent of change and vanguard of revolution and nothing can stop you as a youth, except yourself. It doesn't matter how long it may take for the idea to become a reality. Nelson Mandel was a Creator's idea or solution to the problem of Apartheid in South Africa just like the great deliverer, Moses, was to Israel. The 27 years of imprisonment and other inhumanities done to him could not stop him because Mandela was an idea whose time had come. Your country may not see it that way, but it doesn't stop you. This leads us to the next thing to consider about youth.

6. *Youth is the Greatest Asset of a Nation*

The place of birth of a youth and the fortunes or misfortunes of his family are highly inconsequential in determining the future of the youth if they understand that youth is a time-frame, a season, an awesome responsibility, a predictor of the future and an idea whose time has come, with no external force powerful enough to stop it from becoming a reality. Now, we want to consider youth as the greatest source of wealth and pride of a nation. Any nation that accords her youths a place of honour in the process of nation-building and invests in youthful ideas, history has proven, gets to be far richer and more powerful than oil-rich countries or 'oil-pauperized' nations.

A man was travelling on a journey and his carriage was stalled by mud at a point. A young poor boy who was watching from a distance came and gave him help without asking for anything in return. "What do you want to be when you grow up?" asked the traveller. "I'd like to be a doctor, but I doubt that it will happen since my family does not have the money for such education," the poor boy quickly replied. "Then I will help you become a doctor," said the politician traveller. And as the years went by, the Member of Parliament kept his promise.

Nearly fifty years down the road of history, another famous English statesman lay dangerously close to death due to pneumonia. Winston Churchill had become terribly ill while attending a wartime conference, and England desperately needed his leadership as Hitler threatened to destroy the empire of Britain.

Churchill miraculously recovered because his physician gave him an injection of a new wonder drug called penicillin. Penicillin had recently been discovered by the brilliant medical doctor, Alexander Fleming.

Alexander Fleming was the young boy who pulled the stalled carriage from the mud. And the politician who promised to return the favour by sending him to medical school was Winston Churchill's father, Sir Randolph Churchill.

Randolph Churchill saw what no one else had seen in the face of that young Scottish farm boy. He saw a potential and emergence of a new drug that will save lives from the grips of pneumonia. And his commitment to helping that young man reach his potential saved the life of his own son nearly half a century later. And by saving the life of Winston Churchill, indeed, he may have saved all of England.

How many lives has Nigeria lost because of the short-sightedness of leaders and total neglect of her youths by the government, her politicians and her rich citizens? How many inventions have Nigeria lost because of the greed that has impoverished youths who were sent to make Nigeria an inventing nation by God? How many patents has Nigeria lost to other countries because her youth geniuses left in search of a conducive environment to explore their talents? A case of the internet genius, Philip Emeagwali, comes to mind immediately. How many great inventors, innovators and entrepreneurs were among those two million jobless youths scrambling for mere Immigration jobs because of the poor leadership of a country with over 150 million citizens and 80 million youths? What a youth waste! In my own opinion, Nigeria has the highest rate of dream mortality in the world.

There was a newspaper report that the government of President Goodluck Jonathan earmarked US $1 billion to fight oil theft and pipeline vandalism. It is a good thing to do when you think that oil fields of the Niger-Delta are the greatest source of Nigeria's wealth. However, a better decision could have been made when one considers what Nigeria is losing by just wasting a child in the hand of Boko Haram or getting them crushed in the hands of poverty or is denied of true education. That child could become the Nigerian Alexander Fleming, Bill Gates, Steve Jobs, mention the names of American great inventors, innovators, leaders, entrepreneurs, educators and scientists. Where are Nigeria's own? Compare Nigeria's total assets and those of corporations like Apple, Microsoft, Google, Facebook, IBM, GE, and you will see how poor Nigeria is. These corporations were all ideas of youths. And look at how much revenue they are generating for America while employing millions who, otherwise, would have been unemployed. Compare again how many people the NNPC has employed from its inception and how many employees these corporations currently have in their employs. What if these American youth founders were born in Nigeria? I guess, they would have migrated to America if they were able to escape accidents from our death-traps roads. That's if their minds were not dwarfed by the mediocrities that loom large in our society before they became adults. I mention some of these national challenges not to pull down Nigeria but to tell you that youths of today have great work to do to make Nigeria and Africa truly great.

Youth is an emergence of a new industry that can redefine civilization. The true source of Nigeria's wealth lies in the dreams and aspirations of her youths. Look at how much Nigeria's entertainment industry is generating in terms of revenue and global good will. This is what youth can do if the environment and culture promote creativity and productivity over consumption and poor thinking. Nigeria's national youth football team, for example, is ranked among the best in the world.

An ex-Japanese president said that the one and only asset of Japan is her people. He pleaded with anyone who plans to bomb Japan to give him a day's notice so that he can evacuate his people to a desert. As a way of favour, the President asked the terrorist to pay him a visit after one year and he will see the latest version of technology sitting on a desert! A known business executive from Japan acknowledged that the only asset of Japan is the hard work of her people. My country, Nigeria, will experience greatness equal to her population the day her government prides in investing in her youths over oil exploration! And the generation that will do it is you and this writer. It is our collective responsibility not to bequeath to our children the kind of Nigeria we inherited from our fathers. After all, every good father believes his son will be greater than his achievements. Remember, youth is both a personal and national responsibility. We have no excuse to fail our generation.

The history of inventions and industry in England and America is nothing but biographies of Creativity and profiles in the indomitable spirit of young people. These are youths who explored their creative powers and passions to advance civilizations. They walked their way through poverty to prosperity. They became great and made Britain greater. They became powerful and made America more powerful before the eyes of the world. The contributions of Michael Faraday, Isaac Newton, and other English great minds provided the Americans the foundational catalyst for inventions and innovations which they still display today. Nobody who uses the electric bulb can doubt the contributions of Thomas Edison. Nobody who uses telephone will question the contributions of Alexander Graham Bell. No oil country where Chevron and ExxonMobil operate will doubt the input of John D. Rockefeller to the oil industry, and even to the academic world through his philanthropy. In the 21st century where ICT and mobile apps are like the air we breathe, no sane person will question the contributions of Bill Gates, Steve Jobs, Mark Zuckerberg, and the likes.

If you forget everything I have said so far, I want you to underline this: *You are the greatest asset of Nigeria and Africa*! If you commit to practice what you will be reading in the subsequent chapters, you could be the next source of continental pride for Africa. It is only a matter of time. I am convinced that this century is for Africa to emerge and unleash her creative powers as never witnessed in the history of the world's civilization. And Nigeria is the country to lead the process. Take it or leave it. It is an idea whose time has come!

The story of Abraham Lincoln provides us with a complete set of qualities that can make a young person without any advantage in the world move from the scratch and attain the highest height he dreamed for himself. As a boy, Lincoln predicted his future when he said, at age 10, "I'll be a president." As a youth, he took 100% responsibility for his big dream by reading every book that came his way. By persevering till he won the presidential election, he proved that his presidential dream was an idea whose time had come and nothing could stop it. Lincoln lived like a man with a mission to emancipate the slaves in America while at the same time preserving the union of American States. As a youth, Lincoln saw himself in spite of the crushing poverty that surrounded him, as the greatest asset of America. Above all, Lincoln conquered every obstacle on his way through his unquenchable thirst for knowledge from the cradle until his assassination.

In the next chapter, we'll see how, by sheer power of reading and perseverance, Lincoln started from the scratch and reached his ultimate goal of becoming the president of America.

Chapter Two

THE POWER OF KNOWLEDGE

The Story of Abraham Lincoln's Youth

Inspired knowledge gives you boldness to move into the future with unshakeable assurance of success; it gives you mastery over your limiting environment and circumstances; and it makes you larger than your calling. Nothing is as powerful as a reading youth. Knowledge is power and it has skyrocketed individuals and nations to the Kennedian moon of progress. The prison bars of poverty melt before knowledge because books are your sure window to the world of possibilities. The history of American civilization and the evolution of her democracy is incomplete without the contributions of a poor boy who climbed from the valley of log cabin in a wilderness into the greatest office in America with the ladder of books, perseverance and industry.

A Great Inspiration to Aspiring Leaders

The story of Abraham Lincoln, after more than a hundred years of his death, has inspired many youths who, through the story of his obsession with reading and indomitable spirit of perseverance, have become US Presidents, Senators, Generals and captains of industry. It was the story of George Washington that inspired the young Lincoln to say "Oh, I'll be president," when asked what he would like to become at age 10. What if Lincoln didn't read the "Life of Washington" as a child?

Lincoln's rise from the poorest of log cabins to the White House, to be the President of the greatest republic in the world, is one of the most inspiring stories in American history. Yet he was not a genius, unless a determination to make the most of one's self and to persist in spite of all hardships, discouragements, and hindrances. He made himself what he was—one of the noblest, greatest, and best of men—by sheer dint of hard work and the cultivation of the talents that had been given him. No fortunate chances, no influential friends, no rare opportunities played a part in his life. Alone and unaided, by the grace of God, he lived a great life which will forever challenge different generations of youths across all races.

The story of his life has been told so often that nothing new can be said about him. Yet every fresh reading of the story fills the reader afresh with wonder and admiration at what was accomplished by the poor backwoods boy. One thing his story teaches is that any youth, through the power of knowledge, can rise to any height in life regardless of his or her humble beginnings or environmental disadvantages. How did Abraham Lincoln reach to the top in spite of all odds?

Orison Swett Marden's Account of Lincoln's Childhood and Youth

Let your mind separate itself from all the marvels of the twenty first century. Think of a time when internet, computers, airplanes, mobile phones, railroads and telegraph wires, great ocean steamers, lighting by gas and electricity, daily newspapers (except in a few centres), electronic books and libraries, and the hundreds of conveniences which are necessities to the people of today, were unknown. Even the very rich at the beginning of the nineteenth century could not buy the advantages that are free to the poorest youth at the beginning of the twenty first century. When Lincoln was a boy, thorns were used for pins; cork covered with cloth or bits of bone served as buttons; crusts of rye bread were used by the poor as substitutes for coffee, and dried leaves of certain herbs for tea.

Born into Abject Poverty and the Most Primitive Lifestyle

Abraham Lincoln was born on February 12, 1809, in a log cabin in Hardin County of Kentucky. His father, Thomas Lincoln, was not remarkable either for thrift or industry. He was tall, well built, and muscular, expert with his rifle, and a noted hunter, but he did not possess the qualities necessary to make a successful pioneer farmer. The character of the mother of Lincoln, may best be gathered from Lincoln's own words: "All that I am or hope to be," he said when he was the President of the United States, "I owe to my angel mother. Blessings on her memory!"

It was at her knee he learned his first lessons from the Bible. With his sister Sarah, a girl two years his senior, he listened with wonder and delight to the Bible stories, fairy tales, and legends with which the gentle mother entertained and instructed them when the labours of the day were done.

When Lincoln was about four years old, the family moved from the farm on Nolin Creek to another of about fifteen miles' distance. There the first great event in his life took place. He went to school. Primitive as was the log-cabin schoolhouse, and elementary as were the educational qualifications of his first schoolmaster, it was a wonderful experience for the boy, and one that he never forgot.

In 1816 Thomas Lincoln again decided to make a change. He was enticed by stories that came to him from Indiana to try his fortunes there. So, once more the little family "pulled up stakes" and moved on to the place selected by the father in Spencer County, about a mile and a half from Gentry Ville. It was a long, toilsome journey through the forest, from the old home in Kentucky to the new one in Indiana. In some places they had to clear their way through the tangled thickets as they journeyed along. The stock of provisions they carried with them was supplemented by game snared or shot in the forest and fish caught in the river. These they cooked over the wood fire, kindled by means of tinder and flint. The interlaced branches of trees and the sky made the roof of their bedchamber by night, and pine twigs their bed.

When the travellers arrived at their destination, there was no time for rest after their journey. Some sort of shelter had to be provided at once for their accommodation. They hastily put up a "half-faced camp"—a sort of rude tent, with an opening on one side. The framework of the tent was of upright posts, crossed by thin slabs, cut from the trees they felled. The open side, or entrance, was covered with "pelts," or half-dressed skins of wild animals. There was no ruder dwelling in the wilds of Indiana, and no poorer family among the settlers than the new adventurers from Kentucky. They were reduced to the most primitive makeshifts in order to eke out a living. There was no lack of food, however, for the woods were full of game of all kinds, both feathered and furred, and the streams and rivers abounded with fish. But the home lacked everything in the way of comfort or convenience.

Lincoln, who was then in his eighth year, has been described as a tall, ungainly, fast-growing, long-legged lad, clad in the garb of the frontier. This consisted of a shirt of linsey-woolsey, a coarse homespun material made of linen and wool, a pair of home-made moccasins, deerskin leggings or breeches, and a hunting shirt of the same material. This costume was completed by a coonskin cap; the tail of the animal being left to hang down the wearer's back as an ornament.

This sturdy lad, who was born to a life of unremitting toil, was already doing a man's work. From the time he was four years old, away back on the Kentucky farm, he had contributed his share to the family labours. Picking berries, dropping seeds, and doing other simple tasks suited to his strength, he had so early begun his apprenticeship to toil. In putting up the "half-faced" camp, he was his father's principal helper. Afterward, when they built a more, substantial cabin to take the place of the camp, he learned to handle an axe, a maul, and a wedge. He helped to fell trees, fashion logs, split rails, and do other important work in building the one-roomed cabin, which was to be the permanent home of the family. He assisted also in making the rough tables and chairs and the one rude bedstead or bed frame which constituted the principal furniture of the cabin. In his childhood Abraham Lincoln did not enjoy the luxury of sleeping on a bedstead. His bed was simply a heap of dry leaves, which occupied a corner of the loft over the cabin. He climbed to it every night by a stepladder, or rather a number of pegs driven into the wall.

Rough and poor and full of hardship as his life was, Lincoln was by no means a sad or unhappy boy. On the contrary, he was full of fun and boyish pranks. His life in the open air, the vigorous exercise of every muscle which necessity forced upon him, the tonic of the forests which he breathed from his infancy, his interest in every living and growing thing about him, —all helped to make him unusually strong, healthy, buoyant, and rich in animal spirits.

Lincoln's First Heart-break and Letter before Age Ten

The first great sorrow of his life came to him in the death of his dearly loved mother in 1818. The boy mourned for her as few children mourn even for the most loving parent. Day after day he went from the home made desolate by her death to weep on her grave under the near-by trees.

There were no churches in the Indiana wilderness, and the visits of wandering gospel ministers to the scattered settlements were few and far between. Little Lincoln was grieved that no funeral service had been held over his dead mother. He felt that it was in some sense a lack of respect to her. He thought a great deal about the matter, and finally wrote a letter to a minister named Elkins, whom the family had known in Kentucky. Several months after the receipt of the letter Parson Elkins came to Indiana. On the Sabbath morning after his arrival, in the presence of friends who had come long distances to assist, he read the funeral service over the grave of Mrs. Lincoln. He also spoke in touching words of the tender Christian mother who lay buried there. This simple service greatly comforted the heart of the lonely boy.

Sometime after Thomas Lincoln, his father, brought a new mother to his children from Kentucky. This was Mrs. Sally Bush Johnston, a young widow, who had been a childhood friend of Nancy Hanks. She had three children, —John, Sarah, and Matilda Johnston, —who accompanied her to Indiana. The second Mrs. Lincoln brought a stock of household goods and furniture with her from Kentucky, and with the help of these made so many improvements in the rude log cabin that her stepchildren regarded her as a sort of magician or wonder worker. She was a good mother to them, intelligent, kind, and loving.

His Early Education and Contacts with Books Mostly Borrowed

He was ten years old at this time, and had been to school but little. Indeed, he says himself that he only went to school "by littles," and that all his schooling "did not amount to more than a year." But he had learned to read when he was a mere baby at his mother's knee; and to a boy who loved knowledge as he did, this furnished the key to a broad education. His love of reading amounted to a passion. The books he had access to when a boy were very few; but they were good ones, and he knew them literally from cover to cover. They were the Bible, "Robinson Crusoe," "Pilgrim's Progress," a "History of the United States," and Weems's "Life of Washington." Some of these were borrowed, among them the "Life of Washington," of which Abraham afterward became the happy owner. The story of how he became its owner has often been told.

The book had been loaned to him by a neighbour, a well-to-do farmer named Crawford. After reading from it late into the night by the light of pine knots, Lincoln carried it to his bedroom in the loft. He placed it in a crack between the logs over his bed of dry leaves, so that he could reach to it as soon as the first streaks of dawn penetrated through the chinks in the log cabin. Unfortunately, it rained heavily during the night, and when he took down the precious volume in the morning, he found it badly damaged, all sodden and stained by the rain. He was much distressed, and hurried to the owner of the book as soon as possible to explain the mishap.

"I'm real sorry, Mr. Crawford," he said, in concluding his explanation, "and want to fix it up with you somehow, if you can tell me any way, for I ain't got the money to pay for it with."

"Well," said Mr. Crawford, "being as it's you, Abe, I won't be hard on you. Come over and shuck corn three days, and the book's yours."

The boy was delighted with the result of what at first had seemed a great misfortune. Verily, his sorrow was turned into joy. What! Shuck corn only three days and become owner of the book that told all about his greatest hero! What an unexpected piece of good fortune!

Lincoln's reading had revealed to him a world beyond his home in the wilderness. Slowly it dawned upon him that one day he might find his place in that great world, and he resolved to prepare himself with all his might for whatever the future might hold.

Lincoln Declares and Prepares for His Presidential Ambition

"I don't intend to delve, grub, shuck corn, split rails, and the like always," he told Mrs. Crawford after he had finished reading the "Life of Washington." "I'm going to fit myself for a profession."

"Why, what do you want to be now?" asked Mrs. Crawford, in surprise. "Oh, I'll be president," said the boy, with a smile.

"You'd make a pretty president, with all your tricks and jokes, now wouldn't you?" said Mrs. Crawford.

"Oh, I'll study and get ready," was the reply, *"and then maybe the chance will come."*

If the life of George Washington, who had all the advantages of culture and training that his time afforded, was an inspiration to Lincoln, the poor hard-working backwoods boy, what should the life of Lincoln be to youths of today especially those who live in the dungeon of Africa? Here is a further glimpse of the way in which he prepared himself to be the president of the United States. The quotation is from Ida M. Tarbell's "Life of Lincoln."

The Audacity of Youth

"Every lull in his daily labour he used for reading, rarely going to his work without a book. When ploughing or cultivating the rough fields of Spencer County, he found frequently a half hour for reading, for at the end of every long row the horse was allowed to rest, and Lincoln had his book out and was perched on stump or fence, almost as soon as the plough had come to a standstill. One of the few people left in Gentry Ville who still remembers Lincoln, Captain John Lamar, tells to this day of riding to mill with his father, and seeing, as they drove along, a boy sitting on the top rail of an old-fashioned, stake-and-rider worm fence, reading so intently that he did not notice their approach. His father, turning to him, said 'John, look at that boy yonder, and mark my words, he will make a smart man out of himself. I may not see it, but you'll see if my words don't come true.' 'That boy was Abraham Lincoln,' adds Mr. Lamar, impressively."

Lincoln's father was illiterate, and had no sympathy with his son's efforts to educate himself. Fortunately for him, however, his stepmother helped and encouraged him in every way possible. Shortly before her death she said to a biographer of Lincoln: "I induced my husband to permit Abe to read and study at home, as well as at school. At first he was not easily reconciled to it, but finally he too seemed willing to encourage him to a certain extent. Abe was a dutiful son to me always, and we took particular care when he was reading not to disturb him, —would let him read on and on till he quit of his own accord."

Lincoln fully appreciated his stepmother's sympathy and love for him, and returned them in equal measure. It added greatly to his enjoyment of his reading and studies to have someone to whom he could talk about them, and in after life he always gratefully remembered what his second mother did for him in those early days of toil and effort.

If there was a book to be borrowed anywhere in his neighbourhood, he was sure to hear about it and borrow it if possible. He said himself that he "read through every book he had ever heard of in that county for a circuit of fifty miles."

And how he read! Youths of twenty first century who have books and magazines and papers in abundance in their homes and tons of e-books on the internet, besides having thousands of volumes to choose from in great city and university libraries, can have no idea of what a book meant to this boy in the wilderness. He devoured every one that came into his hands as a man famishing from hunger devours a crust of bread. He read and re-read it until he had made the contents his own.

"From everything he read," says Miss Tarbell, "he made long extracts, with his turkey-buzzard pen and brier-root ink. When he had no paper he would write on a board, and thus preserve his selections until he secured a copybook. The wooden fire shovel was his usual slate, and on its back he ciphered with a charred stick, shaving it off when it had become too grimy for use. The logs and boards in his vicinity he covered with his figures and quotations. By night he read and worked as long as there was light, and he kept a book in the crack of the logs in his loft to have it at hand at peep of day. When acting as ferryman on the Ohio in his nineteenth year, anxious, no doubt, to get through the books of the house where he boarded before he left the place, he read every night until midnight."

His stepmother said: "He read everything he could lay his hands on, and when he came across a passage that struck him, he would write it down on boards if he had no paper, and keep it by him until he could get paper. Then he would copy it, look at it, commit it to memory, and repeat it."

Not Just Reading - He Thought Through and Simplified Every Idea Gathered

His thoroughness in mastering everything he undertook to study was a habit acquired in childhood. How he acquired this habit he tells himself. "Among my earliest recollections I remember how, when a mere child," he says, "I used to get irritated when anybody talked to me in a way I could not understand. I do not think I ever got angry at anything else in my life; but that always disturbed my temper, and has ever since. I can remember going to my little bedroom, after hearing the neighbours talk of an evening with my father, and spending no small part of the night walking up and down and trying to make out what was the exact meaning of some of their—to me—dark sayings.

"I could not sleep, although I tried to, when I got on such a hunt for an idea until I had caught it; and when I thought I had got it, I was not satisfied until I had repeated it over and over; until I had put it in language plain enough, as I thought, for any boy I knew to comprehend. This was a kind of passion with me, and it has stuck by me; for I am never easy now when I am handling a thought, till I have bounded it north and bounded it south and bounded it east and bounded it west."

His Readings Refined His Character and Reflected in His Social Life

With all his hard study, reading, and thinking, Lincoln was not a bookworm, nor a dull companion to the humble, unschooled people among whom his youth was spent. On the contrary, although he was looked up to as one whose educational qualifications in "book learning" had raised him far above everyone in his neighbourhood, he was the most popular youth in all the country round. No "husking bee," or "house raising" or merry-making of any kind was complete if Abraham was not present. He was witty, ready of speech, a good story-teller, and had stored his memory with a fund of humorous anecdotes, which he always used to good purpose and with great effect. He had committed to memory, and could recite all the poetry in the various school readers used at that time in the log-cabin schoolhouse. He could make rhymes himself, and even make impromptu speeches that excited the admiration of his hearers. He was the best wrestler, jumper, runner, and the strongest of all his young companions. Even when a mere youth he could lift as much as three full-grown men; and, "if you heard him fellin' trees in a clearin'," said his cousin, Dennis Hanks, "you would say there was three men at work by the way the trees fell. His axe would flash and bite into a sugar tree or sycamore, and down it would come."

His kindness and tenderness of heart were as great as his strength and agility. He loved all God's creatures, and cruelty to any of them always aroused his indignation. Only once did he ever attempt to kill any of the game in the woods, which the family considered necessary for their subsistence. He refers to this occasion in an autobiography, written by him in the third person, in the year 1860.

"A few days before the completion of his eighth year," he says, "in the absence of his father, a flock of wild turkeys approached the new log cabin; and Lincoln, with a rifle gun, standing inside, shot through a crack and killed one of them. He has never since pulled the trigger on any larger game."

Any suffering thing, whether it was animal, man, woman, or child, was sure of his sympathy and aid. Although he never touched intoxicating drinks himself, he pitied those who lost manhood by their use. One night on his way home from a husking bee or house raising, he found an unfortunate man lying on the roadside overcome with drink. If the man were allowed to remain there, he would freeze to death. Lincoln raised him from the ground and carried him a long distance to the nearest house, where he remained with him during the night. The man was his firm friend ever after.

Women admired him for his courtesy and rough gallantry, as well as for his strength and kindness of heart; and he, in his turn, reverenced women, as every noble, strong man does. This big, bony, tall, awkward young fellow, who at eighteen measured six feet four, was as ready to care for a baby in the absence of its mother as he was to tell a good story or to fell a tree. Was it any wonder that he was popular with all kinds of people?

His stepmother says of him: "Abe was a good boy, and I can say what scarcely one woman—a mother—can say in a thousand; Abe never gave me a cross word or look, and never refused in fact or appearance to do anything I requested him. I never gave him a cross word in all my life. His mind and mine—what little I had—seemed to run together. He was here after he was elected president. He was a dutiful son to me always. I think he loved me truly. I had a son, John, who was raised with Abe. Both were good boys; but I must say, both now being dead, that Abe was the best boy I ever saw or expect to see."

Apart from Books Lincoln Gathered Knowledge by Power of Observation

Wherever he went, or whatever he did, he studied men and things, and gathered knowledge as much by observation as from books and whatever newspapers or other publications he could get hold of. He used to go regularly to the leading store in Gentry Ville, to read a Louisville paper, taken by the proprietor of the store, Mr. Jones. He discussed its contents, and exchanged views with the farmers who made the store their place of meeting. His love of oratory was great. When the courts were in session in Boonville, a town fifteen miles distant from his home, whenever he could spare a day, he used to walk there in the morning and back at night, to hear the lawyers argue cases and make speeches. By this time Lincoln himself could make an impromptu speech on any subject with which he was at all familiar, good enough to win the applause of the Indiana farmers.

So, his childhood days, rough, hard-working days, but not devoid of fun and recreation, passed. Lincoln did not love work anymore than other country boys of his age, but he never shirked his tasks. Whether it was ploughing, splitting rails, felling trees, doing chores, reaping, threshing, or any of the multitude of things to be done on a farm, the work was always well done. Sometimes, to make a diversion, when he was working as a "hired hand," he would stop to tell some of his funny stories, or to make a stump speech before his fellow-workers, who would all crowd round him to listen; but he would more than make up for the time thus spent by the increased energy with which he afterward worked. Doubtless the other labourers, too, were refreshed and stimulated to greater effort by the recreation he afforded them and the inspiration of his example.

Thomas Lincoln had learned carpentry and cabinet making in his youth, and taught the rudiments of these trades to his son; so that in addition to his skill and efficiency in all the work that falls to the lot of a pioneer backwoods farmer, Lincoln added the accomplishment of being a fairly good carpenter. He worked at these trades with his father whenever the opportunity offered. When he was not working for his family, he was hired out to the neighbouring farmers. His highest wage was twenty-five cents a day, which he always handed over to his father.

His First Contact with City Raised His Expectation Higher

Lincoln got his first glimpse of the world beyond Indiana when he worked for several months as a ferryman and boatman on the Ohio River, at Anderson Creek. He saw the steamers and vessels of all kinds sailing up and down the Ohio, laden with produce and merchandise, on their way to and from western and southern towns. He came in contact with different kinds of people from different states, and thus his views of the world and its people became a little more extended, and his longing to be somebody and to do something worthwhile in the world waxed stronger daily.

In March, 1828, Lincoln was employed by one of the leading men of Gentry Ville to take a load of produce down the Mississippi River to New Orleans. For this service he was paid eight dollars a month and his rations.

This visit to New Orleans was a great event in his life. It showed him the life of a busy cosmopolitan city, which was a perfect wonderland to him. Everything he saw aroused his astonishment and interest, and served to educate him for the larger life on which he was to enter later.

The next important event in the history of the Lincoln family was their removal from Indiana to Illinois in 1830. The farm in Indiana had not prospered as they hoped it would, —hence the removal to new ground in Illinois. Lincoln drove the team of oxen which carried their household goods from the old home to their new abiding place near Decatur, in Macon County, Illinois. Driving over the muddy, ill-made roads with a heavily laden team was hard and slow work, and the journey occupied a fortnight. When they arrived at their destination, Lincoln again helped to build a log cabin for the family home. With his stepbrother he also, as he said himself, "made sufficient of rails to fence ten acres of ground, and raised a crop of sown corn upon it the same year."

The Young Independent Lincoln Ready to Face the World as a Man at 21
In that same year, 1830, he reached his maturity. It was time for him to be about his own business. He had worked patiently and cheerfully since he was able to hold an axe in his hands for his own and the family's maintenance. They could now get along without him, and he felt that the time had come for him to develop himself for larger duties.

He left the log cabin, penniless, without even a good suit of clothes. The first work he did when he became his own master was to supply this latter deficiency. For a certain Mrs. Millet he "split four hundred rails for every yard of brown jeans, dyed with white walnut bark, necessary to make a pair of trousers."

For nearly a year he continued to work as a rail splitter and farm "hand." Then he was hired by Mr. Denton Offut to take a flatboat loaded with goods from Sangamon town to New Orleans. So well pleased was Mr. Offut with the way in which Lincoln executed his commission that on his return he engaged him to take charge of a mill and store at New Salem.

There, as in every other place in which he had resided, he became the popular favourite. His kindness of heart, his good humour, his skill as a story teller, his strength, his courtesy, manliness, and honesty were such as to win all hearts. He would allow no man to use profane language before women. A boorish fellow who insisted on doing so in the store on one occasion, in spite of Lincoln's protests, found this out to his cost. Lincoln had politely requested him not to use such language before ladies, but the man persisted in doing so. When the women left the store, he became violently angry and began to abuse Lincoln. He wanted to pick a quarrel with him. Seeing this Lincoln said, "Well, if you must be whipped, I suppose I may as well whip you as any other man," and taking the man out of the store he gave him a well-merited chastisement. Strange to say, he became Lincoln's friend after this, and remained so to the end of his life.

An Honest Youth Determined to Succeed with Pride of Integrity

His scrupulous honesty won for him in the New Salem community the title of "Honest Abe," a title which is still affectionately applied to him. On one occasion, having by mistake overcharged a customer six and a quarter cent, he walked three miles after the store was closed in order to restore the customer's money. At another time, in weighing tea for a woman, he used a quarter-pound instead of a half-pound weight. When he went to use the scales again, he discovered his mistake, and promptly walked a long distance to deliver the remainder of the tea.

Lincoln's determination to improve himself continued to be the leading object of his life. He said once to his fellow-clerk in the store, "I have talked with great men, and I do not see how they differ from others." His observation had taught him that the great difference in men's positions was not due so much to one having more talents or being more highly gifted than another, but rather to the way in which one cultivated his talent or talents and another neglected his.

Up to this time he had not made a study of grammar, but he realized that if he were to speak in public he must learn to speak grammatically. He had no grammar, and did not know where to get one. In this dilemma he consulted the schoolmaster of New Salem, who told him where and from whom he could borrow a copy of Kirkham's Grammar. The place named was six miles from New Salem. But that was nothing to a youth so hungry for an education as Lincoln. He immediately set out for the residence of the fortunate people who owned a copy of Kirkham's Grammar. The book was loaned to him without hesitation. In a short time its contents were mastered, the student studying at night by the light of shavings burned in the village cooper's shop. "Well," said Lincoln to Greene, his fellow-clerk, when he had turned over the last page of the grammar, "if that's what they call a science, I think I'll go at another." The conquering of one thing after another, the thorough mastery of whatever he undertook to do, made the next thing easier of accomplishment than it would otherwise have been. In order to practice debating he used to walk seven or eight miles to debating clubs. No labour or trouble seemed too great to him if by it he could increase his knowledge or add to his skills. No matter how hard or exhausting his work, whether it was rail splitting, ploughing, lumbering, boating, or store keeping, he studied and read every spare minute, and often until late at night.

He now decided to become a lawyer, and devoted his attention, so far as possible, to the accumulation of a thorough knowledge. At one period during his studies he walked, every Saturday, to Springfield, some eight miles away, to borrow and return books pertaining to his studies. These books he studied nights, and early in the morning, out of working hours. In 1834 he was once more a candidate for the legislature, and was triumphantly elected, being re-elected in 1836, 1838, and 1840. In 1837, when he had arrived at the age of twenty-eight, he was admitted to the bar, where he soon became noted as a very successful pleader before a jury.

Application: Books Are Africa's Window to the World of Possibilities
The story of the early life of Lincoln is a masterpiece on the power of reading. Given four hours to cut down a tree, Lincoln said he would use the first three hours to sharpen the axe. No wonder he told Mrs Crawford, "I will study and prepare myself, and then maybe my chance will come". Yes, one day his chance did come in that long presidential debate with Senator Douglass which led to his presidency. It was books that showed Lincoln the possibilities of a world beyond his daily toils in the wilderness. Reading opens your mind to the great possibilities in life and shows you how to follow the footsteps of giants who had journeyed successfully in the field of life. For Lincoln, it was reading the childhood stories of the first president of America, George Washington and that of Henry Clay, the great orator.

Our future is shaped by the books we read and the association we keep as youths. Oliver Wendell Holmes said "Once a mind is stretched by an idea it will never return to its original dimension." Reading a single inspiring book can stretch your mind and dream beyond your imagination. Fredrick Douglas observed that "knowledge makes one unfit to be a slave to poverty and limiting environment. It makes you a creator instead of a creature or a victim of circumstance."

Without the revitalization of reading culture at personal level, the 21st century youths of Africa cannot deal with the multifaceted development issues of today. Without inspired reading, talents and potentials will be wasted. One of the greatest African heroes ever lived, Nelson Mandela, told us that "Education is the weapon with which we can change our world."

Russell Cornwell's advice to the youths is worth pondering here: "Get advice as to the best books to read—a good book is the best of counsellors, for it is the best of some good men; and it is a patient counsellor whom we may continually consult upon the same subject as often as we wish. But waste no time, especially at the opening of your career, upon books which have no message for your manhood and no helpfulness in the work you shall assume for life. When you have once taken up a book as your counsellor, don't put it aside until it has been thoroughly digested and assimilated. One book read is worth a hundred books peeped through; and of all the dilettantes, a literary dilettante is the most contemptible."

No youth can hope to rise above the commonplace who has not made his life a reservoir of power on which he can constantly draw, which will never fail him in any emergency. Be sure that you have stored away, in your power-house, the energy, the knowledge that will be equal to the great occasion when it comes. "If I were twenty, and had but ten years to live," said a great scholar and writer, "I would spend the first nine years accumulating knowledge and getting ready for the tenth."

Lincoln's Advice to Aspiring Youths Who Requested His Counsel
"…If you wish to be a lawyer, attach no consequence to the *place* you are in, or the *person* you are with; but get books, sit down anywhere, and go to reading for yourself. That will make a lawyer of you quicker than any other way."

Readers Become Influential Leaders
As a potential hero and world-changer, you cannot do without good books especially biographies of great minds, history books, and books your profession requires. Read, read, and read until you become a distinguished African leader with global tentacles of positive influence. Empty your purse on your head if you can – it's a guaranteed investment with multiple returns as you march confidently into the future.

The Power of Knowledge

Two things good books will do for you are that they will help you capture a vision for your life and inspire you all the way through the process. In the next chapter, we shall see the power of one unflinching vision in details.

Chapter Three

THE POWER OF ONE UNWAVERING VISION

Africa's future belongs to its young people... We need young Africans who are standing up and making things happen...
— *(US President, Barack Obama)*

Vision: A Defined Hope

Vision is a defined hope for a better future. Hope is a life-sustaining virtue; it is the engine of life. Once this engine is knocked, life becomes a burden too difficult to bear. No situation is too bad or insurmountable until hope is lost. Hope is an invincible power! It is hope that sustains individuals, families, organizations, nations, continents and the entire globe.

Hope is a strong feeling that no matter how bad it looks today, tomorrow will be better, and if it's good today, then tomorrow will bring the best. Hope makes hard work and eventual success possible! It is the reason for waking up early in the morning and retiring late at night. If you keep hope alive, then you keep individuals, families, organizations and nations alive.

Youth is hope. It is the hope of families, organizations, nations and the entire world. Youth is the hope of Africa. A family without a child has limited hope. A nation without youths has no hope. A world without youths has no hope. Just a child is enough to keep a family and nation alive because inside a child are generations yet unborn!

The audacity of youth is the audacity of hope! It is an unshakable belief in a vision not yet realized – a dream not yet actualized — but a necessary ingredient for sustaining life's tempo amidst the disappointments and temporary defeats of today.

The Power of One Unwavering Vision

A Generation on a Mission

The book of wisdom says that people grope in darkness where there is absence of vision for a better life and saner society. The label 'Nigeria' was never in existence until the amalgamation of the Southern and Northern protectorates in 1914 by the British. The first youth generation of Nigeria were young men intoxicated with one vision of securing an independent Nigeria.

As youths, they never enjoyed an independent nation as we have today, rather they fought the battle with all their youthful energies, dynamism, intellectualism, radicalism and delivered a politically-independent nation to us; a journey which started in the 1930s and materialized in 1960. The leading figures among these youths were Dr Nnamdi Azikiwe (The Great Zik of Africa; born 1904), Dr Obafemi Awolowo (The Great Sage; born 1908) and Dr Ahmadu Bello (The Sardauna of Sokoto; born 1909).

As youths, they never enjoyed university education in Nigeria but they worked hard to secure education abroad and gave us indigenous universities. They gave free education to the children and youths. They were not only nationalistic (may be regionalistic) but also Pan-African in their thinking. As young people, they not only worked hard to educate themselves for the future, they also built their own businesses before delving into politics after dismantling the colonial political structures in Nigeria. They were a generation driven by ideology (Awoism and Zikism) and one unwavering vision for national development – political freedom and education for all.

The second youth generation of Nigeria, mainly born in the 1930s, were thorough-bred young intellectuals who blended academic learning with character. A truly courageous set of youths, they handled political power as youths because a generation before them delivered a sovereign nation into their hands. Gen. Yakubu Gowon (born 1934) and Gen. Odumegwu Ojukwu (born 1933) were 33 and 34 respectively when they led the civil war in 1967. In the academia, Prof. Chinua Achebe (born 1930) and Prof. Wole Soyinka (born 1934) were driven by the vision of promoting local cultures and values with the sole aim of restoring Africa's local value system that had been damaged by colonial influence.

While the previous generation fought against political domination, they fought against cultural domination. As pride of Africa and Nigeria, Wole Soyinka was first African to receive the coveted Nobel Prize in Literature and Chinua Achebe was acclaimed to be the father of African literature. A seasoned diplomat and master of elocution, Emeka Anyaoku (born 1933) was the first African to head the Commonwealth for two terms. In the business world, the names of Gamaliel Onosode (born 1933) and Dr Christopher Kolade (born 1932) loom large. This was a generation of perfect gentlemen.

The generations after them cannot be adequately defined with respect to a display of common vision other than a selfish quest for materialism at the expense of national interest. Apart from few distinguished individuals, the dominant features of these generations seem to be self-centeredness and poverty of character. On the contrary, the first and second generations of Nigerians were marked by one feature – vision nurtured through education, driven by courage, and garnished by strength of character.

Faced with the responsibility of rescuing Nigeria and Africa from brinks of decay, the 21st century youth of Africa should be driven by one fixed vision that will benefit Nigeria and Africa. It will demand a consortium of young visionaries driven by the audacity of faith, to unlock the potentials of Africa through the strategic synergy of minds. Do you have a fixed purpose?

One Clear Fixed Purpose: Upsurge of Single-minded Youths

My ultimate desire is to groom crops of young Africans who are sure of their individual purpose in life before entering secondary school and university. Purpose gives direction and meaning to your existence; it controls every decision you make every moment. As man never manufactures a product without a clear purpose in mind, God never creates any person without a definite purpose in mind. Do you know God's purpose for your creation and gifting? It is amazing how many youths, overtaken by social life and avalanche of parties on campuses, forget the main purpose for going to university. In the same way, more than 90% of the human race have forgotten that God has a purpose for sending each person to the world at such a time as the 21st century. Blinded by activity-crowded noisy societies and caught in the web of conflicting people's opinions, majority have lost their individuality and sense of purpose in the 'ocean' of illusory pleasures called the quest for happiness.

As Orison Marden observes, "The man without a purpose never leaves his mark upon the world. He has no individuality; he is absorbed in the mass, lost in the crowd, weak, wavering, incompetent. His outlines of individuality and angles of character have been worn off, planed down to suit the common thought until he has, as a man, been lost in the throng of humanity".

He continues: "There is no grander sight in the world than that of a young man fired with a great purpose, dominated by one unwavering aim. He is bound to win; the world stands one side and lets him pass; it always makes way for the man with a will in him. What a sublime spectacle it is to see a youth going straight to his goal, cutting his way through difficulties, and surmounting obstacles, which dishearten others, as though they were but stepping-stones! Defeat, like a gymnasium, only gives him new power; opposition only doubles his exertions, dangers only increase his courage. No matter what comes to him, sickness, poverty, disaster, he never turns his eye from his goal".

I dare say that any youth who wants to succeed must have a programme. He must fix his course and adhere to it. He must lay his plans and execute them. He must go straight after his goal like a hungry lion. He should not allow himself be pushed away every time a difficulty is thrown in his path. He must be ready to get over or go through it.

There is nothing as common as "unsuccessful geniuses," or failures with "commanding talents" Indeed, "unrewarded genius" has become a proverb. Every generation has unsuccessful educated and talented people. Education is of no value, talent is worthless, unless it can do something, achieve something. But nothing can be achieved without an unwavering concentration on the goal.

What the 21st century (with all its distractions) wants is young men and women who can do one thing without losing their identity or individuality, or becoming narrow, cramped, or dwarfed. Nothing can take the place of an all-absorbing purpose; education will not, genius will not, talent will not, industry will not, will-power will not. The purposeless life will always be a failure in the long run. A college or university education, a head full of knowledge, are worth little to people who cannot use them to some definite end.

Purpose defines everything else, and without it, even the best brain will amount to nothing. But you need to focus without wavering on the object of your BIG PICTURE.

Abraham Lincoln's Unwavering One Goal: To Become the President of America

After reading the 'Life of Washington' by Mason Locke Weems, the young Lincoln was enthralled by the character and greatness of Washington of whom even the great Generalissimo of armies, Napoleon Bonaparte, esteemed. Speaking of Washington in the book, Napoleon Bonaparte said, "The measure of his fame is full. The posterity shall talk of him with reverence as the founder of a great empire when my name shall be lost in the vortex of revolutions." How these words inspired Lincoln to set a fixed goal for himself – TO BECOME THE PRESIDENT OF AMERICA – if possible, become greater than President and General Washington.

It was a firm resolution impossible to be stopped from becoming a reality. The reply of young Lincoln – "I'll study and get ready and then, maybe the chance will come" — shows us that he prepared for his presidential ambition. More than educating himself through books, Lincoln saw conquering obstacles and failures as means of preparing himself for his one fixed vision. He failed in business at age 22; was defeated in the election for legislator at 23; failed in business again at 24; lost his sweetheart at 26; had nervous breakdown at 27; was defeated for Speaker at 29; defeated for elector at 31; defeated for Congress at 34; defeated again for Congress at 39; defeated for Senate at 46; defeated for Vice President at 47; defeated for Senate again at 49 and finally elected for Presidency at 51. It was a journey of forty years but Lincoln wouldn't give up. He refused to be distracted. Did it pay off?

The goal of becoming a president, for Lincoln, was more than an ambition to be great. He viewed being a president as a mere platform to contribute to the greatness of America and to the equality of the human race by kick-starting the process of emancipating the slaves. The greatest accomplishment of President Lincoln was his display of a strong national leadership that saved the union of American states. If Lincoln did not follow through with his presidential dream, the Civil War would have divided

America into two weak countries or more. If Lincoln had given up on his vision, there may not have been any Emancipation Proclamation for the freedom of slaves. Abraham Lincoln is remembered for his highly moralistic, skilful and benevolent leadership. Perhaps, he is one of the most quoted figures in the history of mankind. Do you still remember his famous definition of democracy? "a government of the people, by the people and for the people."

In a book entitled *Rating the Presidents* by William J. Ridings, Jr. and Stuart B. Mclver, more than seven hundred professors, elected officials, historians, attorneys, authors, etc. participated in the poll and rated the presidents. Abraham Lincoln emerged first, Franklin Roosevelt was second, and George Washington was third. The categories in which the various presidents were rated included leadership qualities, accomplishments and crisis management, political skill, appointments, and character and integrity. Lincoln was ranked no lower than first, second, or third in any of the categories, and his overall ranking was first among all American presidents.

In February 2009 another poll sponsored by C-SPAN was released which consisted of a survey of 65 historians. The participants were asked to rank the presidents in ten categories ranging from public persuasion and economic management to international relations and moral authority. Again, Abraham Lincoln came first, George Washington second, and Franklin Roosevelt was third.

Abraham Lincoln's life was anchored on one purpose. He spent his entire life pursuing one vision and goal until it was materialized. In the previous chapter, we saw how he laboured in learning, perseverance and industry, lifting himself from abject poverty to the state of nobility. The goal of sitting in the highest office was something he was determined to reach or die pursuing. The fact remains that he not only became the president but he died a president – president for life! What of you? What is that one goal, with larger impact, you'll tell yourself – it's not over until I win? Just one!

One Life, One vision and One Goal Propelled by Courage

There are two classes of people in every generation as far as history is concerned: the Resource Wasters (RWs) and the Immortal Heroes (IHs).

The Audacity of Youth

The lives of RWs end in the grave but IHs live on after death. RWs are squanderers of life, opportunities, wealth, time and positions. A RW may stay in a political office, say presidency, for eight years and after his demise there is nothing to remember him for, except that he once occupied a position. Such people seek for appointment, not because they have anything to offer but because they need the fame and opportunity the title offers. Or just because they are idle!

On the other hand, IHs invest their lives, time and wealth on one particular vision that will leave the world and people better than they found them. Positions don't make them, they make positions. They are found to be larger than life, their professions and any official position occupied, and at the end, prove to be stronger than death itself. Long after they are dead, every generation quote them, read their books, listen or watch their videos; their businesses still provide jobs, their inventions are still relevant and the institutions they founded stay on from generation to generation. In fact, they are not only institutions of learning themselves, their biographies prove to be the greatest sources of inspiration for the living. Think of Lincoln, Nelson Mandela, Zik of Africa, Obafemi Awolowo, Chinua Achebe, Martin Luther King Jr. Mahatma Gandhi and so on. Each of these names lived for and are known for one thing. Which class do you plan to belong?

Let me share with you a story told by Dr. Robert Gilbert. It is the story of a 10-year-old boy who decided to study judo despite the fact that he had lost his left arm in a car accident.

After three months the boy had begun training with a Japanese judo master, he couldn't understand why his master had taught him only one move. Several months later, the Master took the boy to his first tournament. To his surprise, he won his first three matches.

In the final match his opponent was bigger, stronger, and more experienced. But using his one move, the boy pinned his rival and won the tournament. He became the champion.

On the way home, the boy summoned the courage and asked "Master, how did I win the tournament with only one move?" "You won for two reasons," the Master answered. "First, you've almost mastered one of the most difficult throws in all of judo. And second, the only known defence for that move is for your opponent to grab your left arm." The boy won because

The Power of One Unwavering Vision

he was single-eyed on one particular area and played to his strength, where it is impossible to win him.

To belong to the IHs, all you need is one life, one vision and one goal driven by courage and iron-willed determination. If you stay on this one goal long enough, history will accord you a place in the hall of immortality. Earl Nightingale defines success as 'a progressive realization of a predetermined worthy goal.' What is that one thing you want to be remembered for? What is that one institution you will like to leave behind when you die? For me, my life revolves around youth development. I have been on it for the past ten years!

Know the 'WHAT'; Forget about 'How' and 'When'

When Abraham Lincoln set out to prepare himself for presidency, he had no idea of how long it would take and what he would meet on the road of life. He only knew what he wanted – Presidency or nothing less. When Nelson Mandela set out to fight for the freedom of the blacks in South Africa, he had no inkling on how long or how the journey would be. He only knew what he wanted and was ready to die pursuing that one goal – freedom for all. Abraham Lincoln and Mandela spent 40 and 27 years respectively on the journey before they reached their destinations. It was a case of victory-or-death mind-set. Forget about the 'How,' just know the 'What.' The 'how' will take care of itself.

Get a clear idea of what God wants you to do with your life, and get focused on it. Hold on and run with it. You may pant with desperation sometimes, but don't give up. You are like a bulldog with a bone. Don't allow critics to take it away from you. You are going to need that kind of focused determination in order to keep going when the going gets tough.

Write Down the Vision

What can you see? Where are you going in life? Where do you want to be in the next five, ten, twenty to fifty years? Of what importance are you to Nigeria and Africa? God has great plans for Africa but they can only be actualized through the personal visions of the youths. Africa is called a dark continent not because of the skin colour of its occupants; it is because of lack of young people with vision and courage. We have a pool of energetic talented people without vision. In the physical realm, can you really take a walk with your eyes blindfolded? Sure, you'll need someone to hold your hands and lead you. In the mental realm, if you cannot see the future with your imagination, you go through life blindfolded! The blind Helen Keller said that not having a vision is worse than being born blind.

As a potential leader of industry, you must craft a vision that people will key into. Write the vision down because it will take longer than you expect before it materializes. "No matter how great the talent or efforts, some things just take time. You can't produce a baby in a month by making nine women pregnant," one-time world's richest, Warrant Buffet, observed.

Charting a positive course for the future of Africa requires youth with singleness and tenacity of purpose backed with iron determination. It is for the young courageous fellows.

Get Ready for Battle!

Once you have crafted a vision for your life and your potential organization, and you make up your mind to pursue it until you win, you set yourself up for a battle of destiny. Frankly, inside your big vision are disappointments, temporary defeats, failures, heartbreaks, rejections, discouragements, difficulties, oppositions, neglects, loneliness, and resistance. I have never read of a great achiever who didn't wait longer than he expected before his vision became tangible achievements. You will be tried and refined in the blazing furnace of the truly great. It's going to be tough for you but it is this process that will make you a champion and one of the shining stars of this generation and to the unborn generations. There is no star with a scar!

The good news is that obstacles are your helpers; they are character-moulders and teachers of deeper truth about humanity and the workings of society. Opposing circumstances create strength. Opposition gives us greater power of resistance. To overcome one barrier gives us greater ability to overcome the next. History is full of examples of men and women who have redeemed themselves from disgrace, poverty, and misfortune, by the firm resolution of an iron will. Success is not measured by what a man accomplishes, but by the opposition he has encountered, and the courage with which he has maintained the struggle against overwhelming odds. Not the distance we have run, but the obstacles we have overcome, the disadvantages under which we have made the race, will decide the prizes.

At the end, the story of your struggles and triumphs will be one of the most inspiring soul-lifting stories for generations like we read of Abraham Lincoln and other great minds of ages today.

The obstacles will help you develop the backbone for success. "Three things are necessary," said Charles Sumner, "first, backbone; second, backbone; third, backbone." A good chance alone is nothing. Education is nothing without strong and vigorous resolution and stamina to make one accomplish something in the world. An encouraging start is nothing without a backbone. A youth who cannot stand erect, who wobbles first one way and then the other, who has no opinion of his own, or courage to think his own thought, is of very little use in this world. It is grit, it is perseverance, it is moral stamina and courage that govern the world.

"It is defeat," says Henry Ward Beecher, "that turns bone to flint, and gristle to muscle, and makes men invincible, and formed those heroic natures that are now in ascendency in the world. Do not, then, be afraid of defeat. You are never so near to victory as when defeated in a good cause."

"Every condition, be it what it may," says Channing, "has hardships, hazards, pains. We try to escape them; we pine for a sheltered lot, for a smooth path, for cheering friends, and unbroken success. But Providence ordains storms, disasters, hostilities, sufferings; and the great question whether we shall live to any purpose or not, whether we shall grow strong in mind and heart, or be weak and pitiable, depends on nothing so much as on our use of the adverse circumstances".

Belief in Yourself and Become a Force for Positive Change!

"The greatest battle in life", said Ralph Waldo Emerson, "is the fight to be yourself in the world that is constantly moulding you into something else." The vision you have written down is the blueprint of your true potential but the world won't allow you to have it at a platter of gold. It requires a lion's heart and the fighting spirit of an army general to win the battle. The man without an iron will, says Orison Marden, is "the plaything of chance, the puppet of his environment, the slave of circumstances". If you would succeed up to the limit of your possibilities, you must constantly hold to the belief that you have been equipped for success by God, and that you will be successful no matter what opposes your progress.

The Audacity of Youth

There is something sublime in the youth who possesses the spirit of boldness and fearlessness, who has proper confidence in his ability to do and dare. The world believes in the youth who believes in himself, but it has little use for the timid person, the one who is never certain of himself; who cannot rely on his own judgment, and is afraid to go ahead on his own account.

It is the positive youth who believes that he is equal to the occasion, who believes he can do the thing he attempts, that wins the confidence of the people. He is beloved because he is brave and self-sufficient. Those who have accomplished great things in the world have been, as a rule, bold, aggressive, and self-confident. They dared to step out from the crowd, and act in an original way. They were not afraid to be generals in their fields.

There is little room in this crowding, competing age for the timid, vacillating and drifting youth. He who would succeed today must not only be brave, but must also dare to take chances. He who waits for certainty never wins.

Never admit defeat or allow doubt to sway your mind. Stoutly assert your divine right to hold your head up and look the world in the face; step bravely to the front of whatever opposes, and the world will make way for you. No one will insist upon your rights while you yourself doubt that you have any. Believe in your vision of greatness. Put forth your whole energies. Be awake, electrify yourself, and go forth to the task before you with energetic force! The world steps aside for any youth who knows where he is going.

Make Firm Resolution

Just say "I will" and stand by your resolution, though the hell breaks loose or heaven falls. In his letter to an aspiring lawyer, Abraham Lincoln wrote, "Always bear in mind that your own resolution to succeed, is more important than any other one thing." "There are three kinds of people in the world," says a writer, "the wills, the won'ts, and the can'ts. The first accomplish everything; the second oppose everything; the third fail in everything."

"There are no two words in the English language," wrote Orison Marden, "which stand out in bolder relief, like kings upon a checker-board, to so great an extent as the words 'I will.' There is strength, depth and solidity, decision, confidence and power, determination, vigour and individuality, in the round, ringing tone which characterizes its delivery. It talks to you of triumph over difficulties, of victory in the face of discouragement, of will to promise and strength to perform, of lofty and daring enterprise, of unfettered aspirations, and of the thousand and one solid impulses by which man masters impediments in the way of progression."

An indomitable spirit of will is the test of a young person's possibilities. Can the person will strong enough, and hold whatever he undertakes with an iron grip? It is the iron grip that takes and holds. What chance is there in this crowding, pushing, selfish, greedy world, where everything is pusher or pushed, for a young person with no will, no grip on life? The youth who would forge to the front in this competitive age must be a person of prompt and determined decision.

"It is impossible," says Sharman, "to look into the conditions under which the battle of life is being fought, without perceiving how much really depends upon the extent to which the will-power is cultivated, strengthened, and made operative in right directions."

"The shores of fortune", as Foster says, "are covered with the stranded wrecks of men of brilliant ability, but who lacked courage, faith, and decision, and have therefore perished in sight of more resolute but less capable adventurers, who succeeded in making it to the port".

Will has been called the spinal cord of personality. "The will in its relation to life," says an English writer, "may be compared at once to the rudder and to the steam engine of a vessel, on the confined and related action of which it depends entirely for the direction of its course and the vigour of its movement."

As another writer said: "He who is silent is forgotten; he who does not advance falls back; he who stops is overwhelmed, distanced, crushed; he who ceases to become greater, becomes smaller; he who leaves off gives up; the stationary is the beginning of the end--it precedes death; to live is to achieve, to will without ceasing."

Any youth who desires to secure a place in Africa's history must first teach the world that he is not wood and straw; that there is some iron in him. Youth who have left their mark upon the world have been people of great and prompt decision. The achievements of will-power are almost beyond computation. One talent with a will behind it will accomplish more than a dozen of talents without will-power. Nothing is impossible to the youth who can will strongly and long enough.

Persistence! Persistence!! Persistence!!!

What will make a youth with high hopes, after spending 50 years on earth, amount to nothing? It is the lack of persistence on one fixed goal. The famous quote by the 30th US President, Calvin Coolidge, should be committed to memory, "Nothing in the world can take the place of persistence. Talent will not; nothing is more common than unsuccessful men with talent. Genius will not; unrewarded genius is almost a proverb. Education will not; the world is full of educated derelicts. Persistence and determination alone are omnipotent. The slogan 'Press On' has solved and always will solve the problems of the human race." This should be the slogan of the Rescuer Generation!

The history of the human progress is the story of the triumph of persistence. Every known great figure has had to endure tremendous trials and tribulations before reaching the heights of success and achievement. It is endurance and perseverance which made them great.

"The power to hold on" wrote Orison Marden "is characteristic of all men who have accomplished anything great; they may lack in some other particular way, have many weaknesses or eccentricities, but the quality of persistence is never absent from a successful man. No matter what opposition he meets or what discouragement overtakes him, drudgery cannot disgust him, obstacles cannot discourage him, labour cannot weary him; misfortune, sorrow, and reverses cannot harm him. It is not so much brilliancy of intellect, or fertility of resource, as persistency of effort, constancy of purpose, that makes a great person. Those who succeed in life are the men and women who keep everlastingly at it, who do not believe themselves geniuses, but who know that if they ever accomplish anything, they must do it by determined and persistent industry".

The persistent youth never stops to consider whether he is succeeding or not. The only question with him is how to push ahead, to get a little farther along, a little nearer his goal. Whether it leads over mountains, rivers, or morasses, he must reach it. Every other consideration is sacrificed to this one dominant purpose.

Victory or Death! – Henry Clay

Henry Clay was ambitious, and very early in life, he made up his mind that he would win for himself a more imposing title. While a youth, he dreamed of winning world-wide renown as an orator. Not just a dream, he was DETERMINED to become an ORATOR. Henry Clay later became a brilliant lawyer and statesman and the American Demosthenes who could sway multitudes by his matchless oratory. He once said, "In order to succeed a man must have a purpose fixed, then let his motto be VICTORY OR DEATH."

When Henry Clay, the poor country boy, son of an unknown Baptist minister, made up his mind to become an orator, he acted on this principle. No discouragement or obstacle was allowed to swerve him from his purpose. Since the death of his father, when he was but five years old, he had carried grist to the mill, chopped wood, followed the plough barefooted, clerked in a country store, —did everything that a loving son and brother could do to help win a subsistence for the family.

In the midst of poverty, hard work, and the most pitilessly unfavourable conditions, he clung to his resolve. He learned what he could at the country schoolhouse, during the time the duties of the farm permitted him to attend school. He committed speeches to memory, and recited them aloud, sometimes in the forest, sometimes while working in the cornfield, and frequently in a barn with a horse and an ox for his audience.

In his fifteenth year he left the grocery store where he had been clerking to take a position in the office of the clerk of the High Court of Chancery. There he became interested in law, and by reading and study began at once to supplement the scanty education of his childhood. To such good purpose did he use his opportunities that in 1797, when only twenty years old, he was licensed by the judges of the court of appeals to practice law.

At the age of twenty-seven he was elected to the Kentucky legislature. Two years later he was sent to the United States Senate to fill out the remainder of the term of a senator who had withdrawn. In 1811 he was elected to Congress, and made Speaker of the national House of Representatives. He was afterward elected to the United States Senate in the regular way.

Clay has been described by one of his biographers as "a brilliant orator, an honest man, a charming gentleman, an ardent patriot, and a leader whose popularity was equalled only by that of Andrew Jackson."

Henry Clay's resolution to become a renowned orator regardless of his humble background was more than hundred percent. It was a goal he must achieve or die pursuing.

"I Will Paint or Die!" – The Declaration of a Determined Boy

I will paint or die!" So stoutly resolved a poor, friendless boy, on a far-away Ohio farm, amid surroundings calculated to quench rather than to foster ambition. He knew not how his object was to be accomplished, for genius is never fettered by details. He only knew that he would be an artist. That settled it. He had never seen a work of art, or read or heard anything on the subject. It was his soul's voice alone that spoke, and "the soul's emphasis is always right."

Left an orphan at the age of eleven, the boy agreed to work on his uncle's farm for a term of five years for the munificent sum of ten dollars per annum, the total amount of which he was to receive at the end of the five years. The little fellow struggled bravely along with the laborious farm work, never for a moment losing sight of his ideal, and profiting as he could by the few months' schooling snatched from the duties of the farm during the winter.

Toward the close of his five years' service a great event happened. There came to the neighbourhood an artist from Washington, —Mr. Andrew, whom he overheard by chance speaking on the subject of art. His words transformed the dream in the youth's soul to a living purpose, and it was then he resolved that he would "paint or die," and that he would go to Washington and study under Mr. Andrew.

On his release from the farm he headed for Washington, with a coarse outfit packed away in a shabby little trunk, and a few dollars in his pocket. With the trustfulness of extreme youth, and in ignorance of a great world, he expected to get work that would enable him to live, and, at the same time, find leisure for the pursuit of his real life work. As soon as he arrived Washington, he sought for Mr. Andrew, who, with great generosity, offered to teach him without charge.

The Power of One Unwavering Vision

Then began the weary search for work in a large city already overcrowded with applicants. In his earnestness and eagerness, the youth went from house to house asking for any kind of work "that would enable him to study art." But it was all in vain, and to save himself from starvation he was at length forced to accept the position of a day labourer, crushing stones for street paving. Yet he hoped to study painting when his day's work was done!

Mr. Andrew was at this time engaged in painting the portraits of Mrs. Frances Hodgson Burnett's sons. In the course of conversation with Mrs. Burnett, he spoke of the heroic struggle the youth was making. His client's heart was touched by the pathetic story. She at once wrote a check for one hundred dollars, and handed it to Mr. Andrew, for his protégé. With that rare delicacy of feeling which marks all beautiful souls, Mrs. Burnett did not wish to embarrass the struggling determined boy by the necessity of thanking her. "Do not let him even write to me," she said to Mr. Andrew. "Simply say to him that I shall sail for Europe in a few days, and this is to give him a chance to work at the thing he cares for so much. It will at least give him a start."

In the throbbing life of the crowded city one heart beat high with hope and happiness that night. Her young beneficiary lay awake until morning, too bewildered with gratitude and amazement to comprehend the meaning of the good fortune which had come to him. Who could his benefactor be?

Three years later, at the annual exhibition of Washington artists, Mrs. Burnett stood before a remarkably vivid portrait. Addressing the artist in charge of the exhibition, she said, "That seems to me very strong. It looks as if it must be a realistic likeness. Who did it?"

It was a great work of the poor boy she helped through Mr Andrew anonymously. He has become a successful artist, known in his own country and in England for the strength and promise of his work.

It has been proven that once a person with a fixed dream decides either to perish or succeed in the venture, he automatically enters the league of achievers. This is the fellow the world respects and fears. Nothing can be denied of him who has burnt his bridges. This poor boy knew that the secret lies in knowing exactly what one wants and then allowing events to unfold 'how' without losing hope in the face of the struggles.

Putting It Together

When Paris was in the hands of a mob, and the authorities were panic-stricken, in came a man who said, "I know a young officer who can quell this mob."

"Send for him." Napoleon was sent for; he came, he subjugated the mob, he subjugated the authorities, he ruled France, then conquered Europe.

"Is it *possible* to cross the path?" asked Napoleon of the engineers who had been sent to explore the dreaded pass of St. Bernard.

"Perhaps, it is within the limits of *possibility*" was the hesitating reply.

"*Forward then,*" ordered Napoleon.

The African world yearns for such dauntless courage in order to overcome its present challenges. Africa is looking for young forward-looking Napoleons who are ready to stake their very existence on their purpose. One unwavering vision from an individual African youth backed by iron determination and persistent purpose will transform the future face of Africa. Become part of the Rescuer Generation.

Just start from where you are now with what you have! And this shall constitute the next chapter.

Chapter Four

THE POWER OF SMALL BEGINNING

"There are rooms enough at the top"
— Daniel Websters
"Grave digging is the only venture that starts from the top. Anyone who starts from the top is digging a grave for himself. You don't know how much you can do until you start doing it. You don't know how far you can go until you start the journey."
— David Abioye

See BIG but start SMALL

March 15, 2014 was an unforgettable bloody Saturday for Nigerians and a mournful day for the relatives of about 19 persons who were trampled to death at various exam centres, including national stadium, where about 2 million youths gathered for the job aptitude test organized by the Nigerian Immigration Service. Some reports put the number of the applicants chasing the so-called 4000 vacancies at 6 million.

These multitudes were looking for an employer – a successful leader of an organization. They were searching for the contact of that man who had built his one-man business into a multi-billion-dollar organization capable of paying huge salaries – a man who has paid his dues. You can become such a man or woman. In future your family will need you to meet every need; successful organizations will demand your services and seek for your partnerships; the less privileged will survive through your philanthropy, youths will draw inspiration from your success story; Nigeria will depend on you for provision of employment for her citizens; and Africa will need you to invest in the infrastructural development of the continent.

Behind every successful family, enterprise, organization, country or continent is such an outstanding leader. He is the most valuable person in the society. In the economy, he makes the wheel turn – the entire organization look up to him for leadership and success. This is the man who is responsible for the development of an organization and the growth of the Gross Domestic Product (GDP) of a nation. He's the employer of millions; a dreamer, a planner, a thinker and a doer – the brain behind the movie everyone else watches. As a Government Executive, such a man not only formulates laudable policies but also makes those policies work through strategic implementation. A hard worker who works late in the night and rises very early and when he is not working; he is planning. He is the man who turns dream into reality – theory into practical. He is a practical man.

In the preceding chapter, we established the importance and primacy of having a big dream or a predetermined one worthy goal – a picture of a desirable future that creates passion in you to do everything possible towards its actualization. The great catalyst of human potential, Dr Myles Munroe, after decades of research came to the conclusion that the richest zones on the planet earth are the cemeteries because in there are buried great visions and dreams that were never pursued. I have no doubt in my mind that Africa, in the past and present, had been blessed with people of great potentials, dreams, and extraordinary gifts with capacity to transform it. The missing link has been the dearth of young courageous visionaries capable of translating those potentials into actualities. We need young leaders — people who understand how to produce oak trees from acorns; who know how to plant seeds of possibilities and nurture them into strong institutions. The ultimate need of the hour is the vibrant young leader who not only sees the BIG picture but also has the grit of courage to start SMALL and scale up.

Nature Has Equipped You to Be Such a Leader!

To start small means to start from where you are with what you have. Every big thing starts small. Every big living organism or organization today started as a seed and grew into an influential giant. Think of life itself. What does it take to produce a human person? The process starts with a couple dreaming of having a child. The man and the woman put together what nature has given each, right from where they are. Conception is bound to take place anywhere as long as these seeds meet at the appropriate period. The man or the woman does not need to borrow any human parts to make a child. The nine-month process will produce all the organs and body parts needed. It is called the law of growth. Everything obeys this law. Once the seed is planted and nurtured, growth is inevitable. The big vision you have is a seed which must undergo the law of growth in order to become a gigantic organization. Every successful leader and organization is a product of the process called growth.

E.W. Kenyon wrote, "There is a gold mine hidden in every life. Nature never made a failure. Every man has success hidden away in his soul. No one else can find it but himself. He holds the key to the hidden room. Failure comes because we never sought out the hidden treasure. Failure comes because we tried to find it somewhere else. You can't find it anywhere else. Success, victory and achievement are in you. The exceptional people are those who develop what is within them." You have been equipped and destined for greatness already.

The question is: what do you have in you and around you to start with?

What Unemployment Truly Is

There is virtually no human person without a brilliant idea. The problem or excuse is usually lack of capital. "If only I can find someone who can loan me some money, I will start my own business." The unemployed believes that once a good chunk of cash enters his bank account he will become not just self-employed but an employer of labour. But what is unemployment and capital to start with?

Joblessness is not a physical state; it is a static state of mind. It is a state in which the mind is not usefully engaged. It is a situation in which the mind is not given a target to hit because the owner is waiting for an external force (an employer). Newton's law of motion states that an object remains in a state of rest until a force is applied. You remain unemployed until you employ your mind. The man who will move the world must first move himself. You are not jobless because you have no job. You are jobless because your mind is not working towards a useful end. Your mind is not working because you have not given it a task.

The Audacity of Youth

There are millions of people who are on jobs but in the real sense of it, they are jobless. A man worked as a security guard for 35 years and ended up broke. Another fellow worked as a civil servant for 35 years, he retired and had no idea what else to do with his life. All along, these men were jobless though they were collecting salaries to keep their bodies and souls together. After all, what an employee requires to be paid is mere physical presence from Monday to Friday, apart from public holidays.

By now you should know that joblessness is not a title for graduates alone who couldn't find paid employments. Ninety-nine percent of students in various universities are already jobless under the guise that says – "I will qualify for a good job when I am done with my NYSC." In life, you don't work because you have finished school. Education starts after academic detour or temporary interruptions are over. For this particular reason, Steve Jobs, Bill Gates, Mark Zuckerberg, Henry Ford, Thomas Edison, John D. Rockefeller had to drop out from school since their minds were already engaged with projects that would later change the teaching landscape of the university and create employments for the beneficiaries of formal education.

On the other hand, Google and Yahoo were actually founded by PhD students who turned their academic research papers into business empires. Yerry Yang and David Filo, the founders of Yahoo Inc., had to suspend their academic program indefinitely. These youth founders engaged their minds in an academic environment towards a useful end – to solving an existing problem. They were employed big time by first employing their minds to create something as students. They were so consumed with their self-employment that they had to quit their doctorate program.

Work is a natural process through which humans utilize their creative minds to create value for the benefits of others. It is an opportunity to influence your environment positively with your skill, product or service. You get paid only for bringing value to the marketplace. What value are you creating with your time? Start now to convert your time into value.

You don't earn a living because you have a degree. You earn a living because you have created something that is needed by the market. Lucky you, Nigeria has a large market of about 160 million consumers. You earn a living because you can help existing organizations solve their administrative or business problems. You don't get a job because you have applied for one. You automatically get a job because you have seen a problem within an existing organization which only you have the best solution to.

As much as there are millions of unemployed, the paradox is that every organization, from small to large, is tethering on the brinks of competition. They need young minds who can help out, who can not only show the new way but will lead the way into innovations. There are no more job descriptions to be advertised anywhere in the world, you write your own job description and advertise yourself. This is a brain-based economy. It is a field's day for the knowledge workers. Are you one?

I pity young graduates who are looking for helps from the wealthy people and politicians. In error, they believe that what they need is a 'contact' and they will become instant success. What a bunch of mediocre! They are looking for short-cuts to greatness. In the race of greatness, the lifter is out of order; you must climb the staircase one step after another. You are expected to convert your stumbling blocks into stepping stones and march forward. Success is a progressive realization of a predetermined worthy ideal. It is a journey! The process of the journey is more important than the destination.

The world all over is in search of young entrepreneurs – the youth who creates the jobs for the job-seekers. The person who takes responsibility for the success of others. To such a young fighter, capital is key.

Human Capital: Your Key Resources

What is your true capital? Capital is the initial key resources with which you start an enterprise. Obviously, money is not your initial key resource. If the money is your true capital, why wouldn't you secure it in abundance given the fact that banks have enough cash to dish out? As I studied society, I discovered that people, after making billions of dollars, leave everything behind for the living. Are you part of the living? If yes, then you are qualified to access the money! But you have to make use of your true capital – your wonderful brain, skills and relationship-deserving trust. Money is only a medium of exchange of value.

The key to actualizing your dream is YOU! Capital is the head of a place. The capital of Nigeria is Abuja while that of America is Washington DC, because these are where the Heads of the two countries reside. What is the capital of you? Your HEAD is your true capital.

The head houses your brain, eyes, ears and mouth, and each of them is your key resource. With your eyes and ears you can see or hear about problems that need to be solved. With your brain, you can design the solution to the problem. Most importantly, with your mouth you reach out to somebody who can be of great help to you. It is often said that you're not five people away from the solution you need. What you see and hear will be interpreted and responded to by the way you are. You are the way you are by the way you think. The way you think is determined by what goes into your mind; knowledge is your key resource.

Persuasion is the art of influencing others' decisions with words to your own advantage. The most effective way to do this is by speaking and by showing what you have done with the little you have. The first people to influence are people within your network – family members, friends and colleagues.

Knowledge and relationships you have are enough capital to start an enterprise. If you think you don't have enough of them. Go for knowledge and develop more valuable relationships that will help you become your dream.

The problem is how to use what you already have to get what you don't have. How much do you have in the bank of your mind to withdraw from when you stand or sit before that potential partner or investor? Assuming you have adequate knowledge in your brain, do you have the skill to communicate your value proposition effectively? Before you think of outside help, first ask yourself what can I do on my own? If you do your part very well, you will grow to the next level. It is not how much that is given you that matters, it is how much you can do with the head, eyes, ears, mouth, mind, talents, gifts, the little funds and relationships that have been given you. Starting small means starting with whatever you have, where you are.

Use your head! It is your number one capital. Where can you find the opportunities you are seeking for? One of the greatest truths I ever heard is that you don't see the world and your environment the way they are but the way you think. You interpret reality based on your thinking skill-set. You interpret your environment better when you think better, and you think better when you know better. "The bottle is half full" and "the bottle is half empty" are different interpretations to the same reality. Your response to your environment and the world at large is determined by your interpretation. Seeing opportunities is determined by your interpretation not by your location or the amount of money you have.

You're Sitting on Acres of Diamonds

Around you now are bundles of opportunities that will aid you to start the process of actualizing your written one fixed goal. Can you see them? One of the best-known lectures ever delivered on the surface of the earth, *Acres of Diamonds*, became so popular that the author, Russell Cornwell, delivered it about five thousand times before different audiences in his lifetime.

It is a story of Ali Hafed who lived in a cottage on the river bank, from which he could get a grand view of the beautiful country stretching away to the sea. He had a wife and children, an extensive farm, fields of grain, gardens of flowers, orchards of fruit, and miles of forest. He had plenty of money and everything that his heart could wish. He was contented and happy.

One evening a priest of Buddha visited him, and, sitting before the fire, explained to him how the world was made, and how the first beams of sunlight condensed on the earth's surface into diamonds. The old priest told him that with a mine of diamonds he could purchase a kingdom. Ali Hafed listened, and was no longer a rich man. He had been touched with discontent, and with that all wealth vanishes.

Early the next morning he woke the priest who had been the cause of his unhappiness, and anxiously asked him where he could find a mine of diamonds. "What do you want of diamonds?" asked the astonished priest.

"I want to be rich and place my children on thrones."

"All you have to do is to go and search until you find them," said the priest. "But where shall I go?" asked the poor farmer.

"Go anywhere, north, south, east, or west."

"How shall I know when I have found the place?"

"When you find a river running over white sands between high mountain ranges, in those white sands you will find diamonds," answered the priest.

The discontented man sold the farm for what he could get, left his family with a neighbour, took the money he had at interest, and went to search for the coveted treasure. Over the mountains of Arabia, through

Palestine and Egypt, he wandered for years, but found no diamonds. When his money was all gone and starvation stared him in the face, ashamed of his folly and of his rags, poor Ali Hafed threw himself into the tide and was drowned.

The man who bought his farm was a contented man, who made the most of his surroundings, and did not believe in going away from home to hunt for diamonds or success. While his camel was drinking in the garden one day, he noticed a flash of light from the white sands of the brook. He picked up a pebble, and pleased with its brilliant hues took it into the house, put it on the shelf near the fireplace, and forgot all about it.

The old priest of Buddha who had filled Ali Hafed with the fatal discontent called one day upon the new owner of the farm. He had no sooner entered the room than his eye caught that flash of light from the stone. "Here's a diamond! here's a diamond!" the old priest shouted in great excitement. "Has Ali Hafed returned?" said the priest. "No," said the farmer, "nor is that a diamond. That is but a stone." They went into the garden and stirred up the white sand with their fingers, and behold, other diamonds more beautiful than the first gleamed out of it. So the famous diamond beds of Golconda were discovered. Had Ali Hafed been content to remain at home, had he dug in his own garden, instead of going abroad in search for wealth, and reaping poverty, hardships, starvation, and death, he would have been one of the richest men in the world, for the entire farm abounded in the richest of gems.

No matter where you are right now you are sitting on acres of diamond. Dig deep and exercise patient. Diamonds are never found on the surface. And when they are found, they are to be refined by you for the beauty and value to shine forth.

Michael Angelo found a piece of discarded Carrara marble among waste rubbish beside a street in Florence, which some unskilful workman had cut, hacked, spoiled, and thrown away. No doubt, many artists had noticed the fine quality of the marble, and regretted that it should have been spoiled. But Michael Angelo still saw an angel in the ruin, and with his chisel and mallet he called out from it one of the finest pieces of statuary in Italy, the young David.

If all you can see around you now are problems and lacks, can you bring out the beauty of opportunities in your place by simply going to work on and with them?

Start from Where You Are Now!

The eyes that look are many but the ones that see are very few. Opportunity, says Henry Ford, comes to every man dressed in the overall called work. The present location you are right now is a good place to start from. But can you see the opportunity in people around you and the environment? You are never disadvantaged by your present location. Never you believe that your dream can only be actualized in the big city, in a large digitalized office of an executive; that your big dream is only possible when you have millions of dollars in your account as seed fund. All you need now is what you have; your present location is where you need to be now until you have overgrown it from inside-out. Don't wait for a perfect situation! It doesn't exist.

If a seed is planted in the soil it doesn't say "I'm a big Iroko tree, the ground is too small for me." By the process of growth, the great Iroko starts humbly, staying in the ground for a period of time until it outgrows the ground and sprouts out on the surface. While underneath the ground people trample on it, neglect its potential for greatness and even forget about its existence for years. Remember that Chinese bamboo stays five years underground but in just five weeks it grows to ninety feet tall. It is called humble beginnings. Yes, people will ridicule, mock and neglect you at this stage but you will eventually grow to become all that you have envisioned.

Benjamin Disraeli sprung from a hated and persecuted race; without opportunity, pushing his way up through the middle classes, up through the upper classes, until he stands self-poised upon the topmost round of political and social power. While a youth he envisioned himself swaying his generation with the power of oratory. The first day he stood to make a speech before the House of Commons he was scoffed, ridiculed, rebuffed, and hissed at by his fellow parliamentarians. He simply said, "The time will come when you will hear me." The time did come, and the boy with no chance swayed the sceptre of England for a quarter of a century as its Prime Minister.

If you are in school and all that you have around you are your fellow students; that is a good place to start from. If all you have now is your one-room apartment or a corner in your university dormitory; that is a wonderful place to start from. If all you have around you now are your families or fellow students, they are good people to start with. As soon as you start and continue to grow, you will surely overgrow and become larger than your present environment. Almost all the great corporations and large institutions of the world today can trace their roots from university dormitories, small living rooms, car carriages or even under trees because they could not afford 'a big decent space' and 'high-skilled experienced business executives' at the initial stage.

As a writer I have never written a page without first putting down one word after another until a sentence is made. By increasing the number of sentences I make, a page is produced. By increasing the number of pages I make, a 200-page book is produced. Start with the seed you have from where you are and grow it into an Iroko tree of success.

Apple Inc. Started from a Family Garage

Today iPad and iPhones have become staples in the lives and operations of millions of people the world over. From a college dropout to heading a multi-billion-dollar Apple empire, Steve Jobs dramatically transformed the worlds of personal computing, music and mobile phones, ushering in a new digital era; with some calling him the 21st Century Albert Einstein.

From an early age, Steve Jobs was interested in electronics. As an eighth grader, after discovering that a crucial part was missing from a frequency counter he was assembling, he telephoned William Hewlett, the co-founder of Hewlett-Packard (HP). Hewlett spoke with the boy for 20 minutes, prepared a bag of parts for him to pick up and offered him a job as a summer intern, according to *The New York Times*.

Personal computing was still at nascent stage in Stanford when Wozniak designed the original Apple I computer simply to show it off to his friends in the club. It was Jobs who saw the business opportunity in the computer beyond the excitement of its creator. In early 1976 at ages of 21 and 26 respectively, he and Wozniak, using their own money, began Apple in the Jobs' family garage in Los Altos with an initial investment of $1,300 before securing the backing of former Intel executive A C Markkula, who lent them $250,000. Today Apple is one of the most valuable brands in the world.

It is on record that Jobs never designed a computer in his life. Wozniak was the technical half and Jobs the marketing half of the original Apple I computer. Jobs saw opportunities in his friend Wozniak, he saw opportunities in the club, and began his business from where he was – family garage – with what he has – talents, network of friends, and a paltry $1,300.

Sweet Sensation Started from a Back House

Sweet Sensation is a story of small beginnings. Kehinde Kamson, the founder, started very small with the capital (passion for cooking, her kitchen, her vehicle, management skills, and her husband's support) available to her, from where she was. She spent 8 years in obscurity before she finally established Sweet Sensation as a mere room-and-parlour outlet. Before now she had a wonderful career as the head of accounts unit of an oil-servicing firm with an impressive credential of a chartered accountant having trained with Price Waterhouse Coopers. A graduate of Accounting from the University of Lagos and also alumnus of the prestigious Lagos Business School (Chief Executive Programme), she mustered the gut to quit her juicy job to spend more time with her children.

Right in her home, she saw opportunities. Kamson put her assets together to create opportunity with the enormous time she had as a self-made house wife. For a quiet 8 years, she was baking behind the door, transporting and marketing her products with her small car, and supplying cakes to different individuals and groups. After 8 years of behind-the-door baking, with a 25 square-metre space, 2 used air conditioners and a few scrappy equipment, she started a shop where confectionery would be sold. That was the birth of Sweet Sensation which adorns various roads and streets of major cities in Nigeria today.

It took humility and patience for her to bake in obscurity for 8 years. It took courage and determination for a former chief executive of a department to drive around the town in her car selling cakes. It took vision for her to 'start small' and scale up. Never underestimate what can come out of a small beginning. Just start with whatever you have from where you are, and from there grow up.

From Poor Farm Boy to Founder of Largest Nigerian Legal Firm and World Class Private University

The inspiring story of Chief Afe Babalola is a practical narration of the power of small beginnings and industry. A boy without a chance, he was raised in the farm in a polygamous setting. The poor boy had to fend for his education after passing class six by picking up a teaching job that earned him one pound monthly. Through private study and never entering any university, Afe obtained his B.sc. in Economics and LL.B degree in law (University of London), and later was called to the Bar after his training in Lincoln Inn, London. All of these he achieved while working in a factory in Chelsea.

After arriving Nigeria in 1963 to set up his own law firm, he was faced with a difficult decision – either to follow the path of least resistance by picking a paid job or to face the tough path of self-employment. After fifty years at the Bar, he recalled his experience with *The Guardian*:

"When I came back to this country, it was very tough, seemingly with no light at the end of the tunnel. In fact, since I did not come from a rich family and with the cost of setting up a chamber, people advised me to take up a job with my degrees in Economics and Law. A close friend of mine suggested a number of opportunities, and even brought letters to me, of companies interested in me; I turned them down. I believed in my ability to overcome all problems."

As with any young man who decides to build an enterprise from the scratch, he was faced with the problem of finance. Preferably in his own words: "My first problem was finance; nobody was ready to give me a kobo.... There was nobody in my family to help me. I wrote to a few friends who were working, I asked them to give me a loan of five pounds each and they were six. I was expecting 30 pounds. And I promised to pay back in the next six months. None of them replied." Nothing can stop a determined youth from succeeding. Disappointment and lack of finance would not stop a courageous youth on a mission.

Eventually Afe started his chamber, Emmanuel Chambers, in a garage in Ibadan with only a table, two chairs, a fan, and an imperial typewriter which he acquired on credit and promised to pay by instalments in six months. By the end of the first year he was able to move into a room-and-parlour office. After two years with many briefs coming in, he employed his first two junior colleagues. From that humble beginning in a garage, Emmanuel Chambers has become the largest chamber in Nigeria, with multiple branches across the country and abroad. This little chamber has trained and given opportunities to more than 1,000 lawyers, and has produced more than 70 Senior Advocates of Nigeria (SAN).

Afe revealed, "I have the greatest number of Senior Advocates of Nigeria! I have the largest chamber in Nigeria. Not only that, my chamber has been labelled, 'Kingsway Chamber' because, with our ability, we charge our fees in dollars, the reason is that the naira is not as stable as the dollar... I don't want to mention an appeal case I handled for 14 days and I got my 2 million dollars. I made over N300 billion for a consortium of banks and I got my percentage. I have been handling big cases as far back as 1970."

Apart from his philanthropy and other investments, the little chamber has grown to be the giant temple of legal practice and by virtue of its monumental success, has given birth to a world class university – Afe Babalola University Ado-Ekiti (ABUAD).

Afe Babalola started from a garage with what he had – a sound education, courage and industry. Until date, he still goes to bed at 1 am and wakes up at 5 am. In the true sense of it, he started from the farm with a hoe and cutlass but through a dint of hard work, he walked his way through private study to build two great institutions that will endure for generations. He said, "People will succeed if they have faith in what they are doing. Faith never fails. Faith has component parts – hard work and determination. If you don't have faith in what you are doing, you will never get there...this university is an example of an act of faith. I have faith that the way I planned the institution, the way I planned my chamber, that in 50 years' time, Afe Babalola's chamber will still remain one of the best because of the type of culture we imbibe...that culture has been transferred to Afe Babalola University, Ado-Ekiti – a culture of faith, hard work, industry, humility and good management."

It doesn't matter how big your vision is, and how small you are compared to your ideal. Start with what you have, where you are. I don't care if you desire to be a president, with vision and application of creative energy, you will make it. Barack Obama started from being a community worker, and from there he proceeded to Harvard Law school because he noticed that a law degree would help him achieve his vision of community service. It was in Harvard that he saw the possibility of becoming the American president after winning his election as the first African-American president of Harvard Law Review. Just start and you will meet opportunities on the way alongside with multiple challenges that will themselves make you stronger and bigger if you do not buckle under their weight but turn their experience into valuable lessons.

A Farm Boy That Became a Founder of the Largest Automobile Company and a World Class University in Nigeria

He is called 'Mr Toyota' because he made Toyota products popular in Nigeria through his over 40-year-old company, named Elizade which was coined from his name and wife's name - Elizabeth and Adeojo - during their university days. His full name is Chief Michael Adeojo.

Elizade Ltd is the major supplier of Toyota products in Nigeria, and of recent, has acquired the multibillion-dollar Toyota Nigeria. Like Afe Babalola, Adeojo has also founded a world class university – Elizade University, in Ondo State, Nigeria. The story of 'Mr Toyota' is that of industry from a very humble beginning.

Born into a polygamous family of three wives for a farmer, carpenter and hunter father, Adeojo's chances of getting western education were very slim. With the initial support of his mother, he was enrolled into primary school. He discovered his entrepreneurial acumen as a kid while helping his mother pay his way through school. Before he went to school in the morning, he would hawk pap and in the evening, he would sell kerosene and matches. When he was not selling kerosene or going to farm in the afternoon, he would be pounding and moulding mud for the brick-layers. This was how he survived in his primary school days.

Later with the assistance of his would-be wife and CFAO Motors, he was able to graduate from the University of Nigeria Nsukka with a B.sc in Business Administration. Though the name 'Elizade' was coined during his university days, he did not step out to build his own business until he used what he had – selling skills – to get what he wanted.

Not comfortable with the treatment he received from his employer, British Petroleum (BP), he approached RT Briscoe to appoint him as a freelancer to sell their cars on commission basis. After securing their acceptance, he asked for his annual leave. When it was granted, Adeojo went out selling Toyota cars and within four weeks, he sold 40 cars. He discovered that his commission was more than a year's salary of where he was working as a full-time staff. With this eye opener, he resigned his job. However, it took the intervention of his cousin to convince his wife to allow him to leave his paid job and start his own company. To this he said:

"But my obstacle was how to convince my wife who was not happy because she believed a bird in hand was worth more than 20 in the bush. She was insisting that I should stay back at BP. We both agreed to consult my cousin…We both stated our case and my brother who had earlier done what I did – leaving a paid employment for trading – convinced my wife that she should allow me. That was how we registered Elizade as a company. We started the company at No 71 Awolowo Road, Ikeja. It was our house, office and everything."

He added: "Right from the outset I knew I was a good sales person. I used what I had to get what I didn't have. I used my effort as a sales person to work hard. It was a simple calculation for me."

Can you take an inventory of your assets? How can you use your true capital to start from where you are? Adeojo, the business octopus and University founder, knew that his major capital was his skill and passion for selling, and he explored opportunity from his immediate environment. While on a paid employment, he was looking out for opportunities his environment, skills, relationships, knowledge and experience could offer. When he saw one, he mustered the courage to approach his employer to make a bold demand of his annual leave. He went ahead to display an uncommon courage and faith by calling it quits from a job that provided monthly security for his family.

But what if Afe and Adeojo followed the path of least resistance by holding tightly to paid employment till they lost sight of their dreams because of the fear of starting small? Would there have been two great universities offering jobs for hundreds of academics and other non-teaching staff? Perhaps students in these schools would have stayed back in their homes because of lack of admission in the state and government universities if these two great visionaries did not step out to explore their true potentials in business. What would have happened to those thousands of lawyers who passed through Afe Babalola's chamber, and today are Principals of their own firms – with ripple effects of employing other lawyers? I can't even imagine the number of staff currently working in Elizade Nigeria Ltd and Toyota Nigeria. What if Adeojo stayed cool with BP and probably retired as a Managing Director?

As you reflect, I want you to know that life is not all about your financial success but the impact you could make in people's lives from one generation to another. The institutions these men built have lasted for more than 40 years, still expanding without their direct inputs now, providing jobs and feeding families. You could do same with the principles we have discussed so far. This is how to transform Africa in all facets of life. These two poor farm boys started their enterprises as youths and grew with them. They started with what they had – education, brain, vision, courage, industry, hard work, faith, talents, skills, knowledge – from their immediate environments.

Youths with vision and courage build strong institutions by leveraging the energy, imagination and long time-frame, being a youth offers. Study every successful movement, organization and institution, their stories will not be different from what I have shared with you already. The richest man of today, Bill Gates, had a similar story. Microsoft is a product of two youths who used what they had right from where they found themselves.

Time is a Key Resource You Have

Benjamin Franklin not only understood the value of time, but he put a price upon it that made others appreciate its worth. A customer who came one day to his little bookstore in Philadelphia, not being satisfied with the price demanded by the clerk for the book he wished to purchase, asked for the proprietor. "Mr. Franklin is very busy just now in the press room," replied the clerk. The man, however, who had already spent an hour aimlessly turning over books, insisted on seeing him. In answer to the clerk's summons, Mr. Franklin hurried out from the newspaper establishment at the back of the store.

"What is the lowest price you can take for this book, sir?" asked the leisurely customer, holding up the volume. "One dollar and a quarter," was the prompt reply. "A dollar and a quarter! Why, your clerk asked me only a dollar just now." "True," said Franklin, "and I could have better afforded to take a dollar than to leave my work."

The Power of Small Begining

The man, who seemed to be in doubt as to whether Mr. Franklin was in earnest, said jokingly, "Well, come now, tell me your lowest price for this book." "One dollar and a half," was the grave reply. "A dollar and a half! Why, you just offered it for a dollar and a quarter." "Yes, and I could have better taken that price then, than a dollar and a half now."

Without another word, the crestfallen purchaser laid the money on the counter and left the store. He had learned not only that he who squanders his own time is foolish, but that time itself is a key resource in making money.

Benjamin Franklin's relationship with time should be emulated by anyone who wants to make great a life – a model that can be held up as example for future generations. No wonder, he was known as an inventor, philosopher, scientist, successful businessman and a model President of the United States. He is known with his statement about time; *"Dost thou love life? Then, do not squander time, for that it is the stuff life is made of."*

It's a Matter of Time

The difference between where Africa is today and where it will be in future is time. The difference between where you are today and where you will be in future is time. Time is the distance between your present and future. How you walk that distance will determine the impacts you will make or liability you would constitute to the society.

So far we have discussed starting small with what you have right from where you are, and growing from there. The key factor for growth process is time. It is your key capital. Without the gift of time and health, nothing happens no matter how talented or how much money available to you. So, time is a major resource you have. With time, you can grow a seed into fruit-bearing tree; an idea into a monumental institution; you can change your world. The problem is not availability of time but usability of time. How do you see and relate to time? Don't waste it, it is the stuff the growth of your dream and the change Africa needs is made of.

Putting It All Together

Before you can consider money as an obstacle to your progress, please ask yourself whether you have taken advantage of the following key resources you already have:

- Your wonderful brain (constructive thinking)
- Your knowledge and experience
- Your relationships
- Your skills, gifts and talents
- Your environment
- Your time

By the time you bring these key resources together to build an enterprise, money will show up! Try it and see. It is a lot of work and sacrifice but it is about the lives you will transform and liberate from the clutches of poverty. It is about the contributions you are making for the well-being of the larger society. It is about rescuing Nigeria and Africa from insecurity and criminality posed by jobless youths through job employments your organization will be offering. Think of the next generation, that is how to be big. It is not by accumulations but by contributions.

I invite you to become a part of the Rescuer Generation by spending few minutes with me in the next chapter.

Chapter Five

4J-MODEL PARADIGM-SHIFT: FROM BABY TO RESCUER GENERATION

The Colonial Mind-set

Industrial revolution and the quest to build large empires with strong economic base stirred ambitions in many European nations. They wanted more resources to fuel their industrial production. They competed for Africa as a source of raw materials and as a market for industrial products. In fact, the competition became so fierce that European countries feared war among themselves. To prevent conflict, 14 European nations met at the Berlin Conference in 1884-85 to lay down rules for the division of Africa among themselves. They agreed that any European country could claim land in Africa by notifying other nations of its claim and showing that it had the capacity to control the area. The European nations divided the continent with little thought to the welfare and future of Africa. No African ruler was invited to attend these meetings, yet the conference sealed Africa's fate apart from Liberia and Ethiopia which were free from European control. It is said that three Nigerians, during military era, sat down and divided Nigeria's resources among themselves. Up till date, the writer was told that these men are more powerful than the serving President with all his constitutional powers!

This seizure of a country or territory by a stronger country is called imperialism. As occurred throughout most of Africa, stronger countries dominated the political, economic, and social life of the weaker ones. The only justification for this domination was the belief that Europeans were a superior race than other peoples. The attitude was a reflection of Social Darwinism – a social theory of the time. In this theory, the idea of 'survival of the fittest' was applied to human society. Those who were fittest for survival enjoyed wealth and success and were considered superior to others.

The Europeans considered themselves fittest for survival because of the scientific and technological progress (education) they had made at the time.

No matter what can be said in praise of European world in terms of foreign aid, the psychological onslaught unleashed on the African mind is the primary reason for Africa's under-development. The greatest form of bondage is not the seizure of land and the political machinery of a nation but the programming of the minds of the colonized to view and interpret success in a certain way detrimental to their own freedom, development and growth as a people.

Scramble for Nation's Resources Replaced Scramble for Africa's Resources

More than 50 years after political independence of most African countries, the same spirit of imperialism and pattern of colonization continues to dwarf progress on the continent. The only difference is that where the Europeans sat earlier, the indigenous powers sit today but the same agenda of colonizing the resources of the country for personal deification and building of politico-socio-economic empires continues.

In the same manner the European powers scrambled for the resources of Africa, the political elites continue to scramble for the resources of their own countries through party machineries or military ranks in the case of military regimes. The same selfish motive to build a strong empire with strong economic base is what is driving the politicians to struggle to seize the resources of a country and build personal empires with strong economic base. For example, the so-called powerful people of today in Nigeria are the 'Formers' – people who have used their positions in government to make themselves powerful that almost the entire nation worships them. The spirit of imperialism is the reason for decades of military rule in Nigeria, where the generals used their military powers to seize control of the state's resources with the aim of building personal empires with strong economic bases.

Democracy is still an illusion in Nigeria. Within the political parties, the powerful men hand-pick the candidates. There is nothing as internal democracy in the parties. Almost all the political parties are driven by the same agenda – scrambling for state's resources to achieve a status of personal and political deity. A local government Chairman uses the resources of his constituency to make himself so powerful enough to compete for state's resources at the state's level (governorship). The Governor uses the resources of the state to make himself so powerful enough to compete for presidential election or at least for a senatorial seat. The Minister uses the resources of his Ministry to make himself powerful enough to compete for political seats. The same mind-set and motivation runs from the topmost position to the lowest cadet. (This is my view until APC government proves otherwise through its 'change' ideology)

Beyond the politicians using the resources of the government for personal deification, the culture of imperialism is like lifeblood of our existence. The heads of government institutions simply use the resources of the organizations they oversee for personal gains. Everyone wants to use his little or big office to grab as much as possible. It is this mentality inherited from decades of European imperialism that makes the African man see public offices as an avenue to colonize the common resources for the building of personal wealth and influence. We now call it looting, stealing, siphoning, money-laundering, self-interest...

As I read news in the print media and articles on the social media, as I listen to social commentators on televisions and radios, as I listen to the discussions and analysis of Nigeria's biggest problems by the man on the street especially around newspaper stands, and as I interact with some of the actors in the government theatre, and observe the mind-sets of politicians, civil servants and the 'big fishes' at the helm of affairs of Government's Ministries, Agencies and other Parastatals, I have come to the conclusion that the major challenge confronting Nigeria is corruption, and it is known by all.

They all agreed that Nigeria is blessed with diverse natural resources of which crude oil is but one out of about thirty-four of. In his pocket book, *The Problem with Nigeria*, Chinua Achebe concluded that the problem with Nigeria is squarely that of corrupt leaders. "The attitudes of the people working in organizations," said Earl Nightingale, "will always reflect the attitude of the leader." The cancer of corruption has permeated every fibre of our society. That corruption is a culture in Nigeria is a cliché.

It is all about accumulation, very few think of contribution.

The Baby Generation

As I study further to find out the root cause of under-development in Nigeria, I discovered that the problem has to do with the way the post-independence Nigerians were raised. They were spoiled as youths, and just like any spoilt child, he never grew up to become a man in his thinking. This generation of Nigerians are still 'babies' in their 50s, 60s and some 70s. I call them The Baby Generation because they exhibit the characteristics of a child. They were never taught to be man! They only think of what they can get from Nigeria and never think of what they can give to Nigeria. However, there are still some distinguished honest men and women among them who have given their best to Nigeria.

The Baby Generation never knew what it means to look for an admission into higher institutions for more than a year, neither did they know what it means to look for job opportunities after graduation. They were given free education and enjoyed what they called "bursary allowance" which is largely unknown to my generation. They never struggled for anything in life. In fact, while in the university, companies and government establishments came looking for the best students. They studied hard and were of course more intelligent and learned than my generation, but the purpose of their academic pursuit was wrongly focused. The best student received scholarship to travel abroad for graduate studies, came back to occupy a position in government and from there he relied on government coffers for flamboyant living.

The same colonial mind-set ran in their veins. They never thought of how to survive with their brains beyond creating loopholes in governance for their own personal and selfish gains. They are billionaires but they never produced and exported anything.

Government-Dependent

The Baby Generation were taught to depend on the government for everything – (*national pikins*). The ultimate dream of a youth of that generation was to get a juicy job in government, and then walk his way to the top through promotions by aggressive and all-inclusive lobbying. Government was seen as source of limitless wealth because people in government demonstrated wealthy lifestyles. Everything is provided by the government, whatever government fails to provide, they allocate to themselves.

Hence, as the western world scrambled for the soul of Africa, these generations have scrambled and continue to scramble for the soul of Nigeria – the hen that lays the golden eggs. They called it "national cake." Nigeria is anything but a slice of cake to be shared. Nothing else matters except how to be part of the national cake. They never thought of how to bake the cake. The secret of their monumental success is looting. People who have tasted powerful positions in government have become more powerful than the government itself due to the excess of looted wealth and self-perpetuation they achieved through king-making in politics. What do you expect from a society where the politicians and government officials constitute more than 80% of the wealthy class? Under-development and poverty of the masses! Political wars and domestic 'Berlin Conferences' as seen today.

Personality Worship

Being in government makes you a god – one who has access to untold wealth. Ours has become a society of personality worshippers. Hardly could you find news in newspapers whenever any of these government-made billionaires is celebrating birthday – every page is covered with congratulatory messages from sycophants and beneficiaries of their largesse. Not even Dangote, the richest man in Africa, commands such armies of bootlickers. They are the select few that determine the "success" of others and fate of businesses. They are the lords and masters. We have a bunch of government-made billionaires terrorizing the nation with sirens and entourages of armed forces. They are the black colonial masters. We have powerful personalities but no powerful institutions for human evolvement.

The Society of Babies

The average Nigerian today believes more in government than in himself. He has been trained to look up to government and its officials for success. The civil servant is afraid of retirement because he is afraid of being left on his feet for the first time in his life. He manoeuvres his way to alter his date of birth or years of service so that he will remain on government's payroll longer than required. He was never trained to be a self-reliant man. Nigeria spends 70% of the annual budget to feed these powerful 'babies' and their empires through recurrent expenditures, even the remaining 30% of the capital expenditure are finally looted through conspiracy with external contractors. They have milked Nigeria dry. Majority of them lack values of industry, honesty, integrity and hard work. Their hopes begin and end in the common wealth of 167 million Nigerians.

We are products of our culture. Based on this understanding, these generations may not be blamed for the way they have handled the affairs of the nation. However, the greatest challenge facing my generation is how to transit from a colonial mind-set to a democratic mind-set; how to move from self-centeredness to service-centeredness; and how to move from unearned wealth to value-oriented mind-set. It is to move from the Baby Generation to the Rescuer Generation of nation builders.

4J-Model Paradigm-shift

There is something about the end and the beginning of a new century. People born at such periods are special breeds that initiate paradigm-shift. The political liberators of Africa from colonialism were all born within the first two decades of the 2oth century. The young Africans born within the last decade of the 20th century and first decade of the 21st century will liberate Africa from both the colonial mind-set and the economic dominance of the western world. They are saddled with the responsibility of championing a new type of mind-set after the model of what I call 4J-Model paradigm-shift. It is developed with three biblical characters - Jephthah, Joseph, Jesus, and the philosophy of US President John Fitzgerald Kennedy.

Jephthah

Jephthah was a young mighty warrior but his problem was the circumstances surrounding his birth – he was born of a harlot. He was denied of his inheritance and eventually expelled from his community by his people. But when Israel was confronted with a war challenge from the Ammonites, the elders remembered Jephthah – the man in whose hands lies the solution. They looked for him and begged him to lead Israel.

In the moment of national crisis, tribes, religion, one's background does not matter anymore; it is about the one who has the required skills and leadership qualities that will rescue the nation.

The African continent, especially Nigeria, will develop faster when the older generations accept the reality that the youths are the solution to the problems of the continent. They should reach out to the younger generation who have the skills to rescue the nation from the present decay, regardless of their tribes, religion and circumstances of birth. I don't believe in federal character; I believe in competence character. Young people, on the other hand, must prepare and position themselves as solutions.

Joseph

Joseph was a young man who rescued Egypt and Israel from the doom of economic depression. When the world was about to be hit by great depression it was first revealed to Pharaoh as a puzzle in a dream. The king was disturbed because among his wise counsellors, no one could interpret the dream. The solution was found in Joseph – the Hebrew slave – who was languishing in the prison. The king sought for him, not minding his social status and place of origin because in the moment of national crisis such factors don't matter anymore. He not only interpreted the royal dream but he prescribed the solution. In a few seconds, the slave young man was placed at the position of the Prime Minister of Egypt because he had a solution that would save Egypt and make it the economic hub of the world during the economic downturn.

Actually America uses this model. It is the only nation where immigrants and the children of former slaves have been given the opportunity to lead the country based on what they can offer. Currently, President Barack Obama is of African descent. I have taken time to research the evolution of inventions and technology in America and I discovered that majority of the inventors were immigrants. Take for instance, Alexander Graham Bell – the inventor of telephone – emigrated from Scotland while Albert Einstein – the most powerful man of 20th century – emigrated from Germany. In business, it is the same story. Andrew Carnegie who for decades in the 20th century was the richest man in the world emigrated from Scotland and started work in the United States as a telegrapher without any school education.

Africa will develop faster when it opens her doors for all races and offer a level playing ground for every child to prove his worth, regardless of place of birth. Ours cannot remain a politics of tribe and religion, where the origin of a candidate is of primary importance. The question should be, where would the candidate take us to?. Joseph made Egypt an economic superpower during the global recession, yet he was not just an immigrant but a slave from another country.

Jesus Christ

For three years, Jesus Christ displayed a global leadership that is still spoken of till date. He started with twelve disciples but today he has millions of disciples who call Him Saviour and Lord, including this writer. He washed the feet of His followers and gave up His life for the salvation of the world. He left behind the legacy of servant leadership. The leader must be the servant of the people, and not the ruler over them. He led by positive influence.

Africa will develop faster if the leaders adopt the model of servant-leadership. The most gifted and the privileged must use their resources and skills to serve the people, and not to colonize the resources of the state.

John Kennedy

John Kennedy, elected at 43, remains the youngest elected president of the United States of America. It was cold in Washington, D.C., on Jan. 20, 1961 — a day that would change the lives of many young Americans. It was the day the newly sworn-in President Kennedy delivered his famous inaugural speech. In this speech, the young president challenged the world and Americans to adopt a new philosophy for service with these words:

"And so, my fellow Americans: ask not what your country can do for you — ask what you can do for your country. My fellow citizens of the world: ask not what America will do for you, but what together we can do for the freedom of man."

It was more of a challenge to American youths than a mere speech — it shaped the perception of that generation. One of the youths of that generation, Bruce Birch, recalls "I remember feeling very invigorated by it, feeling at the end of the speech, man, this really makes me want to do something, to contribute." That's what Kennedy's speech was intended to do.

He touched on inspiration in many ways. These are some of the ringing lines from the speech — "the torch has been passed to a new generation of Americans, born in this century.... Now the trumpet summons us again.... In the long history of the world, only a few generations have been granted the role of defending freedom in its hour of maximum danger... I do not shrink from this responsibility — I welcome it."

But none were as direct or memorable as the "Ask Not" line. That was the one that made service an American imperative.

Bruce Birch was only 19 years when Kennedy spoke those life-changing words. He took it to heart and went on to become a teacher, a professor and, later, dean of Wesley Theological Seminary in Washington, D.C. — positions he held for 38 years before retiring.

Another young girl inspired by Kennedy's call for service and contribution to nation's building was Donna Shalala. She was sitting on the floor of her residence hall at Western College for Women in Ohio that January day. The room was packed with freshmen, she remembered, but dead silent as everyone watched on a fuzzy black-and-white television set.

"I could go to graduate school, I could go to law school," she says. "Before I heard the speech I was thinking of being a journalist, a war correspondent as a matter of fact." She remembers feeling like Kennedy wasn't addressing the nation, he was addressing her. And "he was talking about public service," she says.

In 1962, Shalala was one of many young Americans who joined the newly-formed Peace Corps, an organization she called, "the embodiment of President Kennedy's call to our generation for service." Shalala went to a mud village in southern Iran, part of the Peace Corps' first batch of volunteers. All the Iranians knew was that these kids were sent to help by an "energetic young president." For two years she taught at an agricultural college before returning to the U.S. where she earned her doctorate at Syracuse University.

Shalala went on to serve as a professor, president and chancellor at numerous colleges. In 1993, Bill Clinton made her his Secretary of Health and Human Services.

Shalala was only 19 years when President Kennedy spoke those words to her hearing. Fifty years after, she became the president of the University of Miami. She's garnered many honours in her career, the most prestigious in 2008, when then-President George W. Bush awarded her the nation's highest civilian award — the Presidential Medal of Freedom.

The Audacity of Youth

The Co-founder of Lagos Business School - Prof. Pat Utomi - in an interview with Vanguard newspaper, revealed that Kennedy's inaugural speech also shaped his future as a young boy when he said, "...between ages 7-9, I was fed the Kennedy mystic: 'Ask not what your country can do for you, but what you can do for your country.' I read virtually everything the American president said at that time and they've had great effects on me."

The contributions of Pat to the development of leadership and entrepreneurship in Nigeria and Africa cannot be quantified.

Pat Utomi's Story - A Model for the Rescuer Generation

Nothing is so fascinating to a youth with high purpose, life, and energy throbbing in his young blood as stories of men and women who have brought great things to pass. Reading and hearing such inspiring stories is life-transforming – It tells you that you too can do it. It awakens you to take responsibility for whatever you want to become in future. Such was the feeling I had the first time I was in the audience where Prof. Pat Utomi shared the story of his life. That was about six years ago at Full Gospel Businessmen's Fellowship meeting held in Festac, Lagos.

As soon as I got home, I quickly drafted a letter addressed to Prof. Pat narrating how I wished to be great like him in future, having been inspired by his story. The next day I went to Lagos Business School office in Victoria Island to see him but I was re-directed to his Centre for Values in Leadership (CVL) in Surulere. Though I eventually submitted my letter, I did not get any response. May be I wasn't bold enough to follow up, one quality Pat was known for as a youth.

Failure to meet him one on one spurred me to read everything I could lay my hands on about him. And since then, he has been my distant mentor. Though he belongs to the Baby Generation, his life is one of the select few that can be held up as example for youths. He is an embodiment of the qualities we have highlighted so far in this book. In fact, he is a paragon of the 4J-Model – a model for the Rescuer Generation.

"Colonel Garba, I Disagree with Your Position on Angola!"

Pat narrated his experience with Foreign Affairs Minister at age 19. It was a display of uncommon courage of an informed youth. His contact with books assured him that Nigeria wasn't taking its student population into account when formulating major policies, and he wanted to get students to play a critical role in determining the foreign policies of the country which were the most important at the time; being the days of crisis and wars in different African countries.

To communicate his sentiments, he wrote the Foreign Affairs Minister, Colonel Joe Garba, but he received no response. The unrelenting young Pat wouldn't give up. He left Nsukka for Lagos to meet the minister. When told by the minister's secretary, after sizing him from head to toe, to go back to school and direct his letter to his Vice Chancellor through the Dean of Student Affairs, he mischievously quipped, 'who will then send it to God?' Not satisfied with the counsel, he made up his mind to wait for the minister who, fortunately for him was just driving in. With the courage that only the young can muster, Pat roared, "Colonel Garba, I disagree with your position on Angola." The rest was history as that meeting not only brought the minister to his school to debate his position, but as he said, it was the beginning of a life-time friendship between both men.

"The point", said Pat, "is that young people are too willing to accept just anything; everything is taken! Had I listened to the secretary who said I should go back and write… that event might not have happened! … If you wash your hands well, you will eat with old men." How did Pat wash his hands? He read!

He Read Every Single Book in the University Library

Books have proved to be the greatest equalizer of men across races, generations and social classes. They are the windows to the world of possibilities. Only books can expand your possibilities and opportunities in life beyond the limitations of your environment. It was books that helped Abraham Lincoln to see a world beyond the lowly place of his birth in a wilderness. The story of Pat Utomi epitomizes the power of books in shaping the future of a youth. Perhaps, he would have ended up a pilot if not for his early encounter with books while a student at the University of Nigeria, Nsukka.

Pat had entered university just to satisfy his father's advice for him to go to university first before pursuing his ambition of becoming a pilot. The idea was that education would give him an edge over other pilots who didn't have university education. He eventually went to university to satisfy his father, at least to secure his approval for his dream of being a pilot – which was a 'happening' thing for big 'boys' at the time. The story of how he chose his course of study still generates laughter whenever he tells it.

"My going to the University of Nsukka, to me, was simply to have one year of partying, making friends and then go off to aviation school. In fact, a great story was how I chose the course of study; I just closed my eyes, put down the pencil and it turned out to be Mass Communication!" he shared with *Vanguard*.

The historical event that set the tone for the phenomenal 'Professor of Political Economy' as we know Pat today began with a decision to prove his professors wrong, who predicted his impeding failure because of his social lifestyle. He decided to make the university library his 'official room.' It was after the civil war and lots of books were being donated to the university from around the world. His department was given the responsibility of creating a management team for the school library but no student was willing to work voluntarily — they couldn't see the opportunity. After several months the library was closed, Pat volunteered to man the library and in the course of his duty, he devoured every single book on the shelves!

As I said in chapter one, how you spend the season of your youth will determine the outcome of the rest of your life. It was the opportunity to 'dine and wine' with books in the library that made Pat to make up his mind to end up a renowned professor. He is ever willing to express his gratitude to the University authority who trusted him with the key to the treasures stored away in the library.

In his words: "Obviously, the encounter with the library at Nsukka did me a lasting favour in the sense that I continued to develop myself. While in graduate school, my father passed away. Being the oldest of seven children, I needed to return home as soon as possible, so, I had to take on extra loads. Typical graduate load was nine credit hours a semester and strong guys would carry 12, but I carried 15 credit hours! Fortunately, my performance earned me so many grants and I didn't need to take up jobs to foot my bills. After my first semester, every other semester was on one grant or the other. Till date, when you enter my car, it's impossible not to find a book."

4J-Model Paradigm-Shift: From Baby to Rescuer Generation

He further recalled: "As a result of that, at age 26, I had two master's degrees and a Ph.D. As a veritable witness that once upon a time in Nigeria knowledge mattered, at age 27, I held a presidential advisory position in the country."

Pat was a Youth Model of 4J-Model Paradigm!

At age 9, Pat was indoctrinated with President Kennedy's thoughts on the responsibility of youths to national development – "Ask not for what your country can do for you but what you can do for your country." He prepared himself to become a solution to the problems of his society, and a value-provider. At 27, he was called to help his country as a presidential adviser to the-then government of Shehu Shagari – a positioned he qualified by merit, and not by tribe or bribe. He was later called upon to save Volkswagen Nigeria from the major crisis rocking the company as an Assistant General Manager. At 35, after proving his mettle, was appointed the Managing Director of the company – a position he willingly resigned at 38 to make room for upcoming leaders. He wanted to start his own venture from the scratch – he was hungry for a new challenge! Today, he has founded and co-founded successful organizations and institutions.

We Are the Rescuer Generation

Africa needs more Pat Utomis if we must develop this continent. Kennedy's speech is a call for service to our generation too. The torch has been passed on to the Rescuer Generation born in this century and we cannot shrink away from the responsibility staring at our faces. We welcome it. And we recognize that only few generations have been granted the role of defining a continent. With 4J-Model example we can light the African world, and move it from the Third-world status to First-world giant. Now the trumpet summons us to brace up and change our world. As Kennedy pronounced, "The world is very different now. For man holds in his mortal hands the power to abolish all forms of human poverty..." The continent is in our hands now to abolish all forms of poverty, both of mind, spirit and body, as well as political violence.

Men Wanted!

The major challenge confronting us today is that of curbing the "baby mentality." Nigeria needs men. Africa needs men. The world needs men. Diogenes sought with a lantern at noontide in ancient Athens for a perfectly honest man, and sought in vain. In the market place he once cried aloud, "Hear me, O men;" and, when a crowd gathered around him, he said scornfully, "I called for men, not pygmies."

"All the world cries," said Alexander Dumas, "where is the man who will save us? We want a man! Don't look so far for this man. You have him at hand. This man, —it is you, it is I, it is each one of us."

When Garfield was asked as a young boy, "what he meant to be," he answered: "First of all, I must make myself a man, if I do not succeed in that, I can succeed in nothing."

Wanted, a youth who is well balanced, a young man or woman of courage, who is not a coward in any part of his or her nature, who regards his/her good name as a priceless treasure. Wanted, a young fellow who will not lose his individuality in a crowd, young man who has the courage of his convictions, who is not afraid to say "No," though all the world says "Yes." Wanted, a generation who will rescue Nigeria and Africa.

Wanted in Africa today are youths by age but self-reliant men and women in their thinking and contributions. Wanted are value-oriented solution providers; young men and women who are ready to develop themselves and use their skills, knowledge and resources to serve their various countries. Wanted are givers, not takers. At the door post of every organization and institution in Africa is a vacancy ad — "Nation Builders Wanted Urgently!"

I see that nation builder in you. Maybe, being a teenager, you are telling yourself that you are too young to make contributions to the development of Africa. Dismiss that idea right away. Probably, by now your heart is burning and asking: "What can I begin to do today to be part of the Rescuer Generation?" In the next and concluding chapter, I will introduce you to Malala, a Pakistan teenager who is changing the world and influencing global leaders of 21st century. We shall then conclude with things you can start to put to practice now following all we have discussed right from the beginning of this book.

Congratulations! Only a chapter more. Let's wrap it up.

Chapter Six

BECOMING THE 21ST CENTURY'S WORLD CHANGER

It is we who make history, it is we who become the history. So let us make history, bring change, by becoming the change. — Malala Yousafzai

You Are Not Too Young to Change the World — Begin Now!

Friday October 10, 2014 was another heroic day that history will never forget in a hurry. It was the day 17-year-old Malala Yousafzai was pronounced the youngest ever winner of the prestigious Nobel Peace Prize for risking her life for children's rights. Before now, the youngest Nobel Peace Prize winner was Tawakkol Karman at 32. This record has been broken by Malala.

Known as the "Bravest girl in the world", she is the first Pakistan and first teenager to win the award. She was first nominated for the award at 16 and when she lost it she told the BBC: "My goal is not to get a Nobel Peace Prize; it is to get peace." It is to rescue girls from terrorism, poverty and ignorance, to make their voices heard and their plights known to the global leaders. A Rescuer Generation!

Malala was not born into royalty but her selfless struggle has brought her close to the seats of today's powers including presidents of nations, monarchs, Diplomats, business leaders, international media and Hollywood A-listers. She has been named one of the ten most influential people in the world and called "a symbol of hope, a daughter of the United Nations" by the UN Secretary-General, Ban Ki-moon.

Among all the recipients of the 2014 Nobel Prize, Malala's heroism dominated the scene for three reasons: her tender age, her display of courage and her passionate mission to rescue young girls from illiteracy and the crushing hands of terrorists at the expense of her dear life. Her story has become a great inspiration to the world especially among the 21st century youths around the globe.

To call Malala a great girl on account of her age and gender is a grievous injustice to the inspiring story of her heroic struggle to banish illiteracy from the vulnerable world of girls. I chose to call her a "Great Man" because of her audacity in the face of death threat from the bloody terrorists. As a lion is not called the King of the Jungle on account of the size of its body but by the volume of its courage, a real man is not judged by his masculinity but by the strength of his conviction, and how he responded when the fabric of that conviction is tested to the limit. "The ultimate measure of man" said Martin Luther King Jnr., "is not where he stands in moments of comfort and convenience, but where he stands at times of challenge and controversy". This is how to judge the "manness" and the greatness of the Pakistan schoolgirl activist for child's education and peace.

The Audacity of Malala

Malala's hometown of Mingora in Pakistan's Swat Valley was infiltrated by militants from Afghanistan and for a time the whole community was living under the influence of the Taliban. The Taliban set up courts, executed residents and closed girls' schools, including the one that Malala attended. How did she respond to the edict banning girls from attending school? Most people retreated in fear but not Malala, she thrust herself into spotlight to protest against the injustice to her constituency. Her courage of conviction was expressed when in 2008 at age 11 she spoke at a local press club meeting, telling the assembled journalists: "How dare the Taliban take away my basic right to education?" That's an audacity of youth at a crescendo boy!

After the press club speech, she made TV news appearances in both Pakistan and the United States. Using the principle of 'Start from where you are with what you have', under a pen name, she began writing an online diary for BBC about the harsh living conditions of her people under the Taliban rule. After the BBC blog ended, Malala was featured in a documentary made for the New York Times. She also received greater international coverage and was revealed as the author of the BBC blog. Consequently, she began receiving death threats for her outspoken views but she defied the fear of death and magnified the power of her conviction about the right of every girl to receive basic education with peace.

It took the spilling of blood of this courageous teenager at 15 by the terrorist to get the attention of the global leaders, and for Malala to be accorded a place in the golden hall of human 'saviours' not minding her age.

It happened on October 9, 2012 when a masked gunman entered her school bus and asked for Malala by name. She was shot with a single bullet which went through her head, neck and shoulder. Two of her friends were also injured in the process. It was a miracle that she survived the attack.

It is, however, not surprising. As I stated in the chapter one, a youth with a living purpose is an idea of God whose time has come, and there is nothing as powerful as an idea whose time has come. Nothing can stop it from becoming a reality. Malala is an idea of universal education for all children whose time has come. The terrorist's bullets could not stop it.

Malala was not done yet. After her recovery, she grabbed the attention of the world again on July 12, 2013 when she took to the stage at the United Nations' headquarters in New York City and sounded to the hearing of the world that her voice cannot be silenced by the fear of any kind. She spoke with a heart of a lion in the following words:

"They thought that the bullets would silence us. But they failed. And then, out of silence came, thousands of voices. The terrorists thought that they would change our aims and stop our ambitions but nothing changed in my life except this: weakness, fear and hopelessness died. Strength, power and courage was born. I am the same Malala. My ambitions are the same. My hopes are the same. My dreams are the same"

From the choice of her words from the foregoing, you would notice that she has reached the point of no retreat – the principle of win-or-perish – as we saw in the chapter three (The Power of One Unwavering Vision). Her mind was already made up on what she wants. She has crossed the Rubicon. She continued:

"Dear brothers and sisters, we want schools and education for every child's bright future. We will continue our journey to our destination of peace and education. No one can stop us. We will speak for our rights and we will bring change through our voice. We believe in the power and the strength of our words. Our words can change the whole world." Oops! What a courage from a female teenager!

Indeed, the vision, courage, determination and liberating words of little Malala have changed the living conditions of children and have rallied the support of international organizations and global leaders around her cause through Malala Fund. She didn't risk her life for herself alone but for the millions of children who are out of school. Malala is today's example of a Rescuer Generation.

Though still a teenager, she has changed the world. She has made a difference in the world. She started her struggle by expressing her views through blogging right inside her small room. Her story has one strong message to every youth:

"You can achieve anything and you are never too young to change the world".

The World Is Waiting for You

Yes, the world is waiting for you to rise up. The world is in your hands and you can shape it with your dream and courage. You can make a difference in your world and bring change to your industry, community and country. Africa will never remain the same just because you chose to become, in the words of Stephen Covey, "a transition person – one who stops unworthy tendencies from being passed on from prior generations to those that follow." Malala is a transition youth who refused the injustices she suffered to continue with the next generation of girls anywhere in the world. In the process of her struggle, she found her voice in the world. And the world is better today because she spoke! She has made a difference with her life as a youth.

In the lines that follow we shall be dealing with the way forward – how to become a 21st century history-maker and world changer.

Questions to Ponder

How do I begin to make my life count as a youth? How can I find my voice and make my voice heard? How can I separate myself from the crowd and become a powerful positive influence over the crowd instead? How can I become different knowing that until I am different I can never make a difference in the lives of people around me? How do I begin to live and act like a leader and a young role-model? How do I improve myself and affect my family, school, organization, community, country, Africa and the entire world positively as a young person? What decisions and practical steps do I need to take now to start me off on the journey of greatness?

The answers to the above questions are already contained in you. You are a great person. I will only help you raise the awareness of the greatness in you by showing you 6 decisions and practical steps you can take within the next 30 days.

1. Think!

Real thinking means focusing and engaging your mind in a most constructive and productive manner to solve a problem. I must warn you that only few people, less than 5% of humanity, engage their minds in this kind of thinking. It is the hardest job in the world. It requires absolute discipline and sustained focus from the thinker. It is simply tasking your brain on daily basis to provide answers to your questions.

Some decades ago, the late Nobel prize-winner Dr. Albert Schweitzer was asked by a journalist, "Doctor, what's wrong with men today?" The great doctor was silent a moment, and then he said, "Men simply don't think!". And I want to paraphrase: "Youths simply don't think!" To be an agent of change, you must think. All the assignments you will be given here will help you organize your thinking.

Assignment 1:
Get a small notebook with a pen and sit in a place (it may be your room) where nobody will distract you. Be ready to write down anything that comes to your mind as we progress in the next stage of thinking.

2. Reflect!

History makers and world changers are people who solve problems because they care for people. They live a different lifestyle – meeting people's needs and solving life's problems. These are the people that make things happen in every sector of life – in the business world, socio-political world, religious world etc.

The world is besieged by problems. People are facing real challenges in their relationships, businesses and schools. Our environments are dotted with problems. There are enough problems in the society to engage everyone in service to humanity, either for profit-making or for humanitarian purposes. If you take responsibility for the problem of others or the society, you will never be forgotten or live in obscurity. The good news is that you have been cut out and wired to solve a particular problem by God.

That's the purpose of your creation.

Fulfilling this purpose is what Dr David Ogbueli, in his book *The Essence of Life*, refers to as "ministry" and he gave 7 steps to developing your ministry. I have used these steps and they work. Let's use them as a guide for our reflections.

Assignment 2:

    a. Problem Analysis:

Reflect on your environment and identify some of the problems that exist there. It can be your school, the organization or industry you are working in, people in your age-bracket etc. Ask yourself the question: "What are the problems I, persons, or people complain about?" "What are the problems in my town, city, community or country?" If you work in an organization, reflect on the headaches of the organization, many organizations may be facing the same challenge. Identify all the problems that crossed your mind and make a list of them with your pen on your small notebook.

    b. Purpose Identification

Now look at the list you made closely. You will discover that not all the problems you listed out resonate with you. Ask yourself, "Which problem bothers me the most?", "which one am I willing to do something about?", "which problem do I have a burden for?", "which problem from this list do I think I have a passion and capacity to solve?"

Remember, it's just one problem that I am asking you to take from the list. The one that bothers you the most and you have a passion for. In fact, don't worry about whether you have experience, skill and capacity. With passion, they can be developed with time. (This should determine the course you will study in the university in the ideal sense of it.) Write out the problem in a separate page in your notebook.

    c. Project Development

The next step is to ask yourself, "which solution do I have for this problem?", "what is the answer to this question?" "what do I need to package to solve this problem?". The same way you listed out the problems, list out the solutions. Keep the list open because as you read and research further, as you go about your daily business you will begin to see solutions everywhere. In the next 90 days, you should create a solution plan that you can execute right from where you are.

d. Platform Development

After creating the solution plan, you need a platform to execute it. This is where you need to float a business, an NGO, a Movement, a Club that will address the problem. With the help of a mentor, you should find out if the problem will be better solved on the platform of a profit-making enterprise or a social enterprise. If you are already engaged in an organization as an employee, that is your immediate platform except if your idea doesn't fit into the vision of your organization. In that case, you may consider setting up a new platform if you're willing to do what it takes.

Write down the possible names you will call this platform, the service or the product as the case may be. Decide whether you will want to set up your own platform or use an existing platform to deliver your solution. If you are going to use an existing platform, "what platform is that?" Setting up a new platform takes time and it's more difficult than using an existing platform. Bear in mind, not everybody is cut out to become an entrepreneur or employer by setting up their own business or non-profit organization. You may have to function as an employee to execute your plan better. You can speak with your mentor on this further.

e. Potential Analysis

The next step is to ask yourself, "What do I have to solve this problem?" "What are my strengths, my skills?", "Do I have the knowledge and experience?" "What can I do to gain the knowledge and experience I will need?" Analyse fully what you have and what you don't have to solve this problem. This exercise will help you define the kind of people you will network with to complement your efforts.

f. Resource Development

The key set of resources you will need first is human resources. They are people who care about the area that you care about. Ask yourself, "Where can I find them?", "Among my friends, who shares this passion with me, and what role can the person play?"

g. Project Execution

A journey of a thousand miles starts with a step. Ask yourself, "What first step do I need to take now?" Every big thing starts small. In fact, you have already started. Congratulations.

3. Create the picture!

We defined dream as a picture of future that creates passion in you. Having identified your purpose and place in life, it is time to enter the next stage of thinking. It is called imagination. To imagine means to create pictures with your mind.

Assignment 3:

Turn over to a new page in your small notebook and write your answers to these questions: "What level of impacts do I see my platform, product or service making in the lives of people in the next 5, 10, 20 years from now?" "Where do I see myself in the next 30 years in this field or career? "Are there examples of people who have achieved the kind of results I am expecting for myself in the next 10 to 30 years in the same or similar fields?" "What height do I want to attain solving this problem?" "What are my vision and mission statements?" "What do I really want to spend my life doing for the next 30 years?"

You will continue to do this particular exercise until the picture becomes clear and definite. It may at least take you 2 to 5 years!

4. Turn the picture into an obsession!

The reason you have reached this point reading this book is because you have a desire to achieve your dream in life. Now, it is time to turn this dream into a burning desire — a consuming obsession. Until you get to this point, you're not yet ready to do what it takes to be a history maker.

Let your heart burn with the picture you have created for yourself in the preceding step.

Assignment 4:

I. Cut out pictures or print out pictures of at least two history makers in your field and place them where they will always remind you where you are going in the next 10 to 30 years of your life. Let their presence inspire you and motivate action in you. Decorate your room with them. Create an inspiring environment for yourself.

II. Write down on a new page in your small notebook and later transfer it to a small card ONE major goal you want to achieve in line with your vision in the next 12 months. You don't need to show it to anyone, but carry it with you so that you can look at it several times a day. Think about it in a cheerful, relaxed, positive way each morning when you get up, and immediately you have something to work for – something to get out of bed for, something to fight for, something to live for, something to die for if necessary.

Look at it every chance you get during the day and just before going to bed at night. As you look at it, remember that you must become what you think about, and since you are thinking about your goal, you realize that soon it will be yours. In fact, it is really yours the moment you write it down and begin to think about it.

III. Affirm your vision, mission and goal statement with your mouth on daily basis until they are no longer strange to you – until every doubt is rooted out of your heart about their realization. The heavyweight boxer, Muhammad Ali said, "I figured that if I said it long enough, I would convince the world that I really was the greatest." Say it long enough until you convince yourself that you are really the person you have visualized.

IV. Search out for biographies and inspiring stories of great minds and let them inspire you with their words.

"The most powerful weapon on earth is the human soul on fire." — Ferdinand Foch

"Burning desire to be or to do something gives us staying power — a reason to get up every morning or to pick ourselves up and start in again after a disappointment." — Marsha Sinetar

"Desire, burning desire, is basic to achieving anything beyond the ordinary." — Joseph B. Wirthlin

5. Produce a plan for your life!

I believe that God has a plan for your life. Why not find out what the plan looks like? He will show you something. It may not be detailed but it will surely guide your day-to-day choices.

A plan is a proposed or intended course of action with specific timelines. Planning, according to Wikipedia dictionary, is the process of thinking about and organizing the activities required to achieve a desired goal. It is preparing a sequence of action steps to achieve some specific goal.

The ultimate goal is for you to live a great life – exemplary life worthy of emulation in all its ramifications. In the step 2, we dealt extensively on planning your ministry. That's the problem you want to solve for humanity. However, to achieve your ministry or business goals, there are other aspects of your life that must play a major role. For example, personal and leadership development plan, relationships and marriage plan, financial plan etc.

Assignment 5:
In your little notebook, try to also answer the following questions:
- *Personal and leadership development*

"When do I want to finish my university education and what course should I study?"

"What university and why that school?" "Why should I study that course?" "What can I do daily to improve my spiritual life?" "What can I do daily to improve my mind?" "What can I do daily to remain healthy?" "What can I do to bring out the leader in me?"

Remember, a plan is a specific action steps. So write down specific books you will read, specific trainings you will attend, specific exercises you will do. Attach specific timeline to each.

- *Relationships and marriage*

"How can I expand the network of valuable friends in my life?" "What is the criterion for choosing a friend for me and what are the boundaries?" "When do I want to get married?" "What shall be my criterion for choosing a worthy wife or husband?" "Do I meet this standard myself?"

- *Financial and asset*

"When do I hope to make my first one million Naira (or dollar depending on the currency of your choice)?" "What kind of service will I give to attract this money?" "What can I do daily to improve my market value?" "What can I do to increase my financial literacy level?" "What kind of assets do I want to have in the next 5 to 10 years?"

I must warn you – don't be in a hurry to accumulate wealth. It is built with time. So be fair with yourself in writing down the amount you desire and the timing attached to it. You are still young!

6. Resolve!

Resolve means promising yourself that you will never give up. It is burning the bridges behind you. It is giving yourself no room for retreat or surrender. Benjamin Disraeli, the great British statesman, once said, "Nothing can resist a human will that will stake even its existence on the extent of its purpose." In other words, when someone truly resolves to "do or die," nothing can stop him. We saw that in chapter three of this book. You may have to visit it again and again.

Assignment 6:
Ask yourself, "How long am I going to work to make my dreams come true?" I suggest you write, "As long as it takes," That's what it will take to see you through this journey. Write down again, "I will never give up until I win."

Turn to a fresh page in your little notebook and do an agreement between you and the problem you want to solve for humanity. State clearly that you will never give up on this project no matter how long it takes. In that agreement, make God a witness number one. You can have a close friend, a mentor or a relative as a second witness, who will hold you accountable to this covenant.

Finally, commit this agreement to God in prayer. Ask him to help you stay through the process. With God nothing is impossible!

Final Word

For over a decade I have been studying the lives of great men and great women who have written history with their lives and I discovered that they were ignorant of three things at a time in their journey of self-actualization.

1. They were totally ignorant of how big their dreams will turn out to be when actualized at the very point of dream conception. When achieved, a dream is always bigger than the initial thinking of the dreamer. It will happen to you too.
2. They had no idea of what it will take to actualize their dreams. It never crossed their minds about the level of sacrifice they would eventually make, the disappointments, rejections and loads of work awaiting them. They had no idea about where the resources will come from – the wonderful people that will come their way to help them achieve their dreams and where the money will come from. It will happen to you too.
3. They had no idea about how long it will take for their dreams to become verifiable facts. It usually takes longer than planned for. It will happen to you too. Don't be surprised.

On the contrary, they were sure of this one fact: "It's possible". They had absolute faith that their dreams will become a fact one day. They didn't care about any other factor. They looked up to God and depended on divine providence to achieve their lofty dreams. Truly, nothing is impossible to a person who believes. Believe in God who alone can see you through to the end. Believe in your dream too. Believe that you can do.

If you believe God and do whatever it takes, it will happen for you. I want you to do one more assignment for me. Close your little notebook and write the below statement on the front cover page boldly:
"IT'S POSSIBLE!"

"During my lifetime I have dedicated myself to this struggle of the African people. I have fought against white domination, and I have fought against black domination. I have cherished the ideal of a democratic and free society in which all persons live together in harmony and with equal opportunities. It is an ideal which I hope to live for and to achieve. But if needs be, it is an ideal for which I am prepared to die."

— **Nelson Mandela**

"I may, therefore, have said something indiscreet. I have said nothing but what I am willing to live by and, if it be the pleasure of Almighty God, die by."

— **Abraham Lincoln**

"Like anybody, I would like to live a long life. Longevity has its place. But I'm not concerned about that now. I just want to do God's will. And He's allowed me to go up to the mountain. And I've looked over. And I've seen the Promised Land. I may not get there with you. But I want you to know tonight, that we, as a people, will get to the Promised Land!"

— **Martin Luther King Jnr.**

ACKNOWLEDGEMENTS

THANK YOU FOR KEEPING MY HOPE ALIVE

As a young man with humble beginnings, countless individuals, academic institutions, organizations and chains of events have helped to keep my hope alive – to keep my vision of Africa alive. Books, audio-visual materials and stories of heroes, both dead and living, have shaped my thought-pattern. It is an impossible venture to mention all the names. This book is a proof of your positive influences on my young impressionable mind.

Worthy of mention, however, are organizations that sowed the seed of this research work in my heart.

Thank you *Federal Ministry of Youth and Sports* (FMYS), Nigeria for enriching this revised edition through your review and further encouragement. Worthy of mention are the Honourable Minister, Mr. Solomon Dalong (Congratulations sir!), Mr. Luka J. Mangset (Director, Enterprise Development and Promotion), and Mr. Ida Isa Sumaia (Chief Youth Development Officer).

Thank you *National Universities Commission* (NUC), Abuja for your inputs especially the Executive Secretary, Professor Julius A. Okojie, who wrote the Foreword. This would not have been possible without the assistance of Mrs. Constance Goddy-Nnadi (Director, Executive Secretary's Office).

Thank you the *African Independent Television* (AIT) for believing in me and for the platform you gave me on several occasions to express my views on youth and national development, especially Ada Onyechere whose comment on one of those occasions sparked off the thought processes, making this book a reality.

Thank you *Nigerian Television Authority* (NTA) for the platform you gave me - only very few media outfits of your standing can risk featuring an inexperienced youth on a live network program at the time you did.

Thank you *Family Ministries International* under the leadership of Pastor Sarah Omakwu for rekindling my passion especially at those moments it seemed all hope was lost.

Thank you the *African Policy Research Institute* (APRI) under the leadership of Amb. S.T. Dogonyaro (OON) for providing me with the research facilities and conducive atmosphere to start and finish this work.

Thank you all my young and brilliant reviewers from secondary schools, universities and NYSC for your sacrifices and valuable inputs. Your thoughts have made this edition more youth-friendly.

Published works of Orison Swett Marden of blessed memory have been helpful in putting together some of the stories and insights that make up this book.

Thank you Elvis Iyorngurum, for going through the initial script and for your editorial inputs. I heard the news of your sudden death at the point of concluding this edition and I was shocked. Rest in peace my editor and good friend.

Thank you, my esteemed reader, for the interest you have shown by picking up or clicking on this book in spite of tons of other good books competing for your attention. I hope to have an exciting journey with you in the pages ahead.

Let all the glory and praise be given to the Almighty God who brought these wonderful people to my world to help me when it mattered most in Jesus' name.

CONNECT WITH US

The long-awaited dream to set up a platform for all-inclusive empowerment of youth of Africa has become a fact. It's our pleasure to introduce *Inspire Youth Africa* (IYA) to you and also invite you to connect with us through our website and Facebook page (www.inspireyouthafrica.org and www.facebook/InspireYouthAfrica respectively).

IYA is a home for the energetic youths on mission with a living purpose. It's a place you can draw the inspiration to dream more, learn more, become more, do more and lead better. It's all about youths with clear vision and an invincible courage to change the narrative of Africa.

We would also love to receive your feedback on the book (The Audacity of Youth) you have just read via: audacityreaders@gmail.com

If you want the author to speak at your youth conference, seminar or workshop, you can also contact him through the same email or +2348094932236.

You can also visit: www.tochiokafor.com.ng

www.ingramcontent.com/pod-product-compliance
Lightning Source LLC
Chambersburg PA
CBHW051655040426
42446CB00009B/1150